I0008193

Internet for Everyone

Internet for Everyone

Reshaping the Global Economy
by Bridging the Digital Divide

EMDAD KHAN

InternetSpeech, Inc

iUniverse, Inc.
Bloomington

INTERNET FOR EVERYONE
RESHAPING THE GLOBAL ECONOMY
BY BRIDGING THE DIGITAL DIVIDE

Copyright © 2011 by Emdad Khan.

All rights reserved. No part of this book may be used or reproduced by any means, graphic, electronic, or mechanical, including photocopying, recording, taping or by any information storage retrieval system without the written permission of the publisher except in the case of brief quotations embodied in critical articles and reviews.

iUniverse books may be ordered through booksellers or by contacting:

iUniverse
1663 Liberty Drive
Bloomington, IN 47403
www.iuniverse.com
1-800-Authors (1-800-288-4677)

Because of the dynamic nature of the Internet, any web addresses or links contained in this book may have changed since publication and may no longer be valid. The views expressed in this work are solely those of the author and do not necessarily reflect the views of the publisher, and the publisher hereby disclaims any responsibility for them.

Any people depicted in stock imagery provided by Thinkstock are models, and such images are being used for illustrative purposes only.
Certain stock imagery © Thinkstock.

ISBN: 978-1-4620-4251-7 (sc)
ISBN: 978-1-4620-4250-0 (hc)
ISBN: 978-1-4620-4249-4 (ebk)

Library of Congress Control Number: 2011914241

Printed in the United States of America

iUniverse rev. date: 08/10/2011

Contents

Foreword

The means of communication across international borders has been made easier through the use of the Internet service. To all intents and purposes, this is an amazing invention through which humanity is able to discover knowledge and exchange information by the use of the computer, yet it has certain limitations and challenges in terms of accessibility particularly in societies where the computer is not common place, and the English language is not in use generally. This being the case, the need for a user friendly service became imperative so that as many people can have access to the Internet.

I have learnt by reading this book that in a world of growing rich-poor gap, widening Digital Divide, increasing social exclusion and unavailable healthcare for the Bottom of the Pyramid people (BOP), it is important to address these issues from a practical new perspective. Dr. Emdad Khan's book describes an effective method of bridging the Digital and Language Divides by talking and listening to the Internet using any phone, called **Voice Internet**. The key technical contribution **Voice Internet technology** has brought to the industry is "**rendering**" that allows content to be transformed from today's website into **Short, Precise, easily Navigable, Meaningful and pleasant to listen to content in real time.**

His book **"Internet For Everyone: Reshaping the Global Economy by Bridging the Digital Divide"** also tells us how to go **beyond bridging the Digital Divide** and improve **economic, social, cultural and other developments by focusing on education, innovation and entrepreneurship.**

The book addresses the key reasons for widening Digital Divide and shows how the Voice based access and its associated "rendering" capability overcomes most of the issues associated with the current methods. To name a few: phone is ubiquitous, especially with the phenomenal increase in access to mobile phone among the BOP, relative to both computers, and high end phones and Personal Digital Assistants (PDAs); talking and listening does not require literacy, very prominent at the bottom of the pyramid; unlimited access to any website as opposed to the need to re-write websites into small web pages to fit on a small screen; easier to learn and use; and usable while mobile.

Dr. Khan has introduced a new divide called **Language Divide**, similar to the Digital Divide and of equal magnitude. Over 70 percent of Internet content today is in English. Thus, many people in non-English speaking countries are left out from major part of the Internet which is called the Language Divide. This Divide has not been talked about much in the literature. The book provides a nice practical solution to the Language Divide by translating the content from English into other languages (and from any language to other languages) in real time and reading it over any phone. In fact, the Digital Divide will not be fully bridged if the Language Divide is not bridged as well.

The book emphasizes that Voice Internet is an **enabling technology**. The core technology can be used to develop many new products and services including: **MicroBrowser** allows any website content to be automatically and effectively displayed on any cell phone or PDA screen at ease **without the need to re-write** the web content in another language; **Voice Computer** allows a user to store, edit and manipulate files etc. on a server via phone call; **NetTalk** allows VoIP call using no broadband phone or no broadband connection, and more. These are all very important products for the Bottom of the Pyramid people (BOP).

My experiences in helping many people at the bottom of the pyramid (BOP) in Zambia and Africa give me very good confidence on the approaches proposed by Dr. Khan, especially to transform bottom of the pyramid people into an **enormous resource** by bringing the Internet to almost everyone having some access to a phone and then providing education, innovation and entrepreneurship and involving all the key players in the food chain including the Governments, Non-Governmental Organizations (NGOs), service providers, organizations, universities, and research institutions using a good "Business Model". Dr. Khan also emphasized using all existing successful methods including telephone infrastructures, existing websites as they are, existing service providers and existing financing models such as Microfinance. *These are very convincing and compelling approaches to really transform BOP into an enormous resource.*

The focus on education, especially, on the informal education is very important. Many BOP cannot afford to go to school, many rural areas do not have sufficient number of schools or sufficient number of teachers and other resources. Getting a formal education may take long time and many may still not get jobs. On the other hand, some quick informal education, e.g., on. "how to preserve mangoes" can help many people. And such education can be provided easily over the phone using the Voice Internet. Dr. Khan nicely tied up Internet access, education, innovation and entrepreneurship to create an enormous resource from the BOP—"*utilize the access to information to knowledge, use knowledge to drive innovation & entrepreneurship to finally drive the development. Education is a key component to develop knowledge from the information. It is also a key component for innovation and entrepreneurship*".

The book also proposes logical solution to the problem of rich getting richer and poor getting poorer. Basically, the world is controlled by rich people (corporations or individuals).

So, the whole financial system is based on mainly to preserve rich people's interest. Thus money mainly flows among the rich people and from the poor to the rich people; very little or no money flows from the rich to the poor. By creating an enormous resource from the BOP, rich would start using such a low cost valuable resource, causing significant amount of money to flow from the rich to the poor in a sustainable way which is very much needed to practically minimize the rich-poor gap.

Moreover, the newly created resource from the BOP will start creating new companies, new products and services, many of which will be attractive to the rich as well as Khan explains. Thus, more money will flow from the rich to the poor. The poor would buy much less things from the rich. These, in turn, will help achieve the United Nations Millennium

Development Goals (MDGs). These would also help circulate most of the money within the poor. Accordingly, the rich-poor gap will be minimized in a sustainable way, and many poor will be out of poverty, many will have great prosperity and some will even become rich. Together, they can start re-shaping the global economy.

Minimizing the rich-poor gap and improving the economy of the BOP will result significant improvements in other key areas including **social, cultural, political and global peace.** Accessing the Internet can stimulate key informal education to base of the BOP—people can naturally talk, listen and learn. People will be busy in learning as it will help them in various ways, most importantly their economic condition. Once they learn some good stuff and get a jobs, they will be more busy with their jobs and possibly with more continued learning. Hence they will be less interested in destructive activities such as terrorism. Besides, there are various other key added benefits—once base of the pyramid people get out of the poverty, all poverty related issues will be minimized or eliminated totally. Key poverty related issues are terrorism, spreading diseases, committing various social crimes, refugees from the developing world, disruption of law & order, not advancing education, healthcare, social depression and the like. Thus, by letting base of the Pyramid people get out of poverty and help drive global economy, this will in turn greatly help achieve **global peace.**

Internet For Everyone: Bridging the Digital and Language Divides—A Reality is an essential handbook for anyone who has the determination and vision to make a difference in a practical way to bridge the **Digital & Language Divides, help improve economic, social, cultural and other developments and world peace.** The approaches presented are powerful, practical and effective. This book is particularly a must read by policy and *decision makers in the Government and non-Government Organizations (NGOs), Civil Societies, Organizations, Foundations, Corporations, educators, students, entrepreneurs, innovators and also the rich individuals, especially, those who would like to help the many Bottom of the Pyramid people around the world.*

Kenneth D. Kaunda Dr (GCEZ)
FIRST PRESIDENT OF THE REPUBLIC OF ZAMBIA

Preface

Why I wrote this Book

The world wealth is distributed very unevenly (e.g. top 1% of rich people own 40% of the world wealth!). Various gaps exist in today's world: Rich-Poor gap, Digital Divide gap, Language Divide gap, gap in natural resources, gap in ethnicity and many more. More importantly most gaps have been increasing consistently in general. So, myself and my team at InternetSpeech, Inc, the company that I founded in 1999, have dedicated the last decade to understand why these gaps are increasing and how such gaps can be minimized. I realized that existing schemes to bridge the Digital Divide are good but not sufficient, and will not be able to really bridge the Divide. Learning from the users of Voice Internet (the technology that I invented to practically bridge the Digital Divide) and the industry, I also realized that just bridging the Digital Divide will not be sufficient—we also need to bridge another Divide of equal importance, the Language Divide. Moreover, just bridging the Digital and Language Divides will not be sufficient—we also need to focus on Education, Innovation and Entrepreneurship to really minimize all gaps and significantly help Economic, Social, Cultural and other developments with significant positive impact on world peace. Converting the Bottom of the Pyramid People (BOP) into an enormous resource is the key, and we need to provide them Internet and Education using the most natural interface (voice & hearing) ; using the most ubiquitous device, a simple phone and avoiding the need to know how to read or write. BOP are poor from financial standpoint but not from intelligence standpoint. So, given the time, efforts and guidance, they can be converted into a huge resource; thus helping themselves as well as the rich people as rich people will have access to low cost enormous expertise.

So, I have written this book to share this story.

In this world of over 6.5 billion people, more than 4 billion people are poor—40% live in poverty, and 16% live in extreme poverty. The World Bank defines poverty as living on less than $2 a day and absolute or extreme poverty as living on less than $1 a day. Nobel Laureate Joseph Stiglitz in his fascinating latest book "Making Globalization Work" [Stiglitz2006] says "Think for a minute what it means to live on one or two dollars a day. Life for people this poor is brutal. Childhood malnutrition is endemic, life expectancy is often below fifty years, and medical care is scarce. Hours are spent each day searching for fuel and drinkable water and . . . .". Apart from inadequate income two other issues are heavily associated with people living below the poverty line: **insecurity and powerlessness.** One World Bank report published a nice statement from a young poor woman in Jamaica that captures the sense of powerlessness: "Poverty is like living in jail, living under bondage, waiting to be free". In general, poor have few opportunities to speak out. When they speak, no one listens; when someone does listen, the reply is that nothing can be done; when they are told something can be done, nothing is ever done.

On the other side of the coin there are the rich people, much smaller in number, but they own over 80% of the world wealth!!! They enjoy all the benefits of the civilization, they control the world economy, they control world business, world laws—they control almost everything except poverty. Well, that is not quite true though. They try to minimize poverty by donation, philanthropy, foundations etc. Obviously that is not enough since poverty has been increasing over centuries. In 2004, the United Nations took a new initiative to minimize poverty and improve the global distribution of wealth. This is called the Millennium Development Goals (MDG). Many people are working together to achieve this worthwhile global dream by 2015. It is important to take a closer look at the differences between rich and poor nations, and rich and poor communities within nation states. How does one rank the differences and gaps as to their contribution to sustaining poverty and preventing a sustained migration out of poverty. What are the causes for these gaps, what are the types of these gaps, are there other similar gaps, can these gaps be bridged, and if so how, to what level and the like.

Broadly speaking, the inequality is inherent in mother-nature. The world natural resources were not uniformly distributed when the world was created, different races were born in different parts of the world inheriting different resources and opportunities, not every human is born with the same capabilities, not every human develops the same level of intelligence even under the "same" environment etc etc. In short, by birth we are all different, the equity is different from the beginning. So, as we grew as a human race more gaps and inequities got developed. Today, we have rich-poor gap, gap in natural resources, gap in ethnicity, gap in male-female capabilities, gap due to the computer revolution (the so called Digital Divide), the gap due to disabilities and so on. Even a much simpler gap exists, between students in a class. Assume that a class has all the good equipments like a computer for each student, a nice projector so that everyone could easily see the lecture notes and everyone could hear the teacher very well—after providing all these facilities to all students, not all students in this class will perform equally. This implies that even if we do our best to minimize all the gaps, because of its inherent property, some gaps will remain. That is why Darwin said "only the fittest will survive".

Should we try to reduce all these gaps? Can we really make these gaps go away? If so, how can we do so? These are the few key issues we will discuss throughout this book. Our premise is that the gap is an inherent property in this world. So, not all gaps can be eliminated or reduced to the same degree. For example, natural resources—a country cannot just acquire its missing natural resources. We have some good control on some gaps and relatively less control on other gaps. The Digital Divide, for example, is a gap that can be reduced to a manageable level that will have a measurable impact on a multifaceted program to reduce the gap between rich and poor. Yes, bridging the Digital Divide will eventually help reduce the gap between the rich and poor but there are many other factors that contribute to the rich-poor gap.

In general we should try to minimize all the gaps—no questions about that. But we would need to set our expectation right—that there will be some gaps no matter how much we try to minimize it as it is inherent in the system. **However, by lowering it to a good level and to continue lowering it will yield a better world and hence that should be our goal.**

We will limit the scope of this book to the issues with the Digital Divide and Language Divide (over 70% of the Internet content today is in English;

thus, non English speaking people are left out from the major part of the Internet which is called the Language Divide) ONLY and their impact on other gaps, including **how bridging the Digital Divide and Language Divides can really change World economy; but we are not going to specifically address issues related to how to bridge other gaps.**

The existing approaches of bridging the Digital Divide are good but not sufficient to truly bridge the Digital Divide. The existing approaches of bridging the Digital Divide can be broadly classified into two groups:

(a) by providing computers or low cost simple computers or computer like devices and Internet connectivity to people who do not have one
(b) by providing personal devices like PDA and cell phone with Internet connectivity

As of latest market data, there are about 550 million connected computers as opposed to over 5 billion (over 4 billion wireless and over one billion wire-line phones [LinkCBSNews]). Thus, computers represent only 14% of telephone population on the average worldwide. This ratio is even worse in the developing countries. Improving this ratio to a desirable number, especially, in developing world would take long time. Additionally, certain population (like elderly, blind, visually impaired people and people unfamiliar with computers) would have difficulty in learning how to use a computer and Internet. Many cannot easily learn how to use a computer and Internet. The drop out rate from computer training schools worldwide is over 30%. Even some people who are reasonably familiar with computers are having difficulty in keeping up with the requirement to learn new things like how to deal with pop-ups, viruses, spam filters, registry edits and the like.

Personal devices like a cell phone or PDA are great devices to communicate via voice or text with small content. But these are not good devices to do computing or to access the Internet. The key reasons are:

(a) Difficult user interface because of small screen and small keypad. In fact, these devices are getting smaller, in general, whereas our eyes and fingers are not.

(b) The content is limited as one would need to re-write the content in another language like WML (Wireless Markup Language) in case of cell phone viewing; or the content needs to be scrolled in case of a PDA.

(c) Visual access makes such devices difficult in an eyes busy-hands busy situation like while driving.

(d) Visual access mechanism makes it unusable by people who cannot read or write.

Today about 15% of the cell phone have browsing capability and ready for Internet access. It will take number of years before all cell phones will have screen-based Internet access and some computing power. Even if they all have computing power and screen based Internet access, many people will not be able to use them because of the reasons mentioned above. And many would not be able to afford them.

Thus, existing approaches will minimize the gap but are not sufficient to truly bridge the Digital Divide. On the other hand **Voice Internet and Voice Computer** (explained in detail in this book) can truly bridge the Digital Divide to anyone who has some type of telephone—wire-line phone, wireless phone, PDA and the like. Voice Internet and Voice Computer do not need a computer. Users basically make a phone call and an automated attendant allows the caller to access the Internet and enjoy surfing, searching, email, e-commerce and other features. Users basically talk and listen to the Internet. In other words, the telephone becomes the browser. In Voice Computer, a user calls a phone number (like the Voice Internet) and an automated attendant allows user to access and edit files, move files between directories, create/manage directories and the like, in a virtual computer. Simply stated, the telephone becomes the computer. Voice Internet and Voice Computer can provide the benefits of the Internet and computer to over 5 billion people who have access to some type of phone. Voice Internet overcomes the difficulties mentioned above with existing approaches:

- no need to buy a special device (thus allowing easy access to many more people)
- no need to deal with small screen or small key pad as users basically talk and listen

- much easier to learn as learning how to use a phone is much simpler than learning how to use a computer or personal device
- no need to re-write the content in another language. There are over 3 billions of websites on the Internet. Re-writing all of them would be cost prohibitive and hence not practical
- no need to learn how to read or write

The other key challenge that Voice Internet overcomes is the "rendering" problem. The Internet was designed with visual access in a large display device in mind. Thus, all the information is laid out that attracts our eyes but not ears. Rendering or converting such information into **short, precise, easily navigable, meaningful and pleasant to listen to content is a very hard problem that Voice Internet has overcome.** These key features of rendering are very important as when listening, one does not have time to listen to everything on a page, would like to move around easily and quickly and make sure that content heard is the content that was desired.

An **Automated Attendant** (also called an **Intelligent Agent, IA**) is used to perform the "rendering" function. IA performs rendering by

(a) automatically generating important information of the page, called, "Page Highlights", presenting them in a small amount of information at a time that one can easily follow.
(b) finding appropriate as well as only relevant content on a linked page selected by a Page Highlight, assembling the relevant content from a linked page, and presenting them.
(c) and providing easy navigation.

Rendering allows users to easily navigate within and between pages using simple voice commands or keypad entries. The Intelligent Agent is capable of learning user's preferences, to continually improve ease of access and usage over time.

Rendering is achieved by using algorithms similar to the algorithms used by sighted users. The key steps of rendering are done using the information available on the visual web page itself and employing appropriate algorithms to use all such information including text content, color, font size, links, paragraph, amount of texts and meaning of the words. Some language processing algorithms are also used to further refine the rendering, navigation and filling of on-line forms (Form Filling). This is similar to how the brain of a normal sighted person renders information from a visual page by looking into the font size, boldness, color, content density, link, meaning of titles/labels, and then selecting a topic; going to the desired page and then reading only the relevant information on the desired page. Form filling is done by presenting forms as Form Page Highlights and also creating appropriate questions, taking the text/voice inputs from the user and then filling and submitting the form.

Thus, a user can seamlessly access any content on the Internet, interact with any forms and complete transactions like shopping, banking etc. using a simple phone and his/her own voice. Another key feature is that the **content can be translated in real time into another language**, providing audio access to, for example, English-language web pages for those with limited English language skills.

Voice Internet is an **enabling technology**. The core technology can be used to develop many new products and services including **MicroBrowser** (to allow any website content to be automatically and effectively displayed on any cell phone or PDA screen at ease) **without the need to re-write** the web content in another language, **Voice Computer** (to allow a user to store, edit and manipulate files etc. on a server via phone call), **netTalk** (allowing VoIP call using no broadband phone or no broadband connection) and more.

What's next after the Digital and Language Divides are bridged from Connectivity Standpoint? Let's assume that together with conventional methods of using computers, PDAs, cell phones, and the proposed method of Voice Internet, the Digital and Language Divides are really bridged from connectivity standpoint. Now what? Well, the benefit of getting into the Internet needs to be utilized properly to really help meet basic needs including food, shelter, education, communication, health, business and economy. That in turn will help minimize the gap between rich and poor. To really bridge the Digital Divide, we will need to address the other key factors: utilize the access to information to knowledge, use knowledge **to drive innovation & entrepreneurship** to finally drive the development.

Education is a key component to develop knowledge from the information. It is also a key component for innovation and entrepreneurship.

Many of the difficulties that hinder economic development in the under-developed and developing countries can be eased with Internet based education and business. Education with focus on entrepreneurship and innovation can jump start the economy of these countries. For example, countries moving up the food chain in manufacturing (like China) has to outsource lower level tasks to other countries, like Vietnam. Many other countries can copy this process without too much efforts. Similarly, India is trying to moving up the food chain in software and service related businesses. Many developing countries can do the same. China and India are two good examples that played the game in the right way and hence in fact became a friend of the countries controlling the world. The same is also true for Japan and Israel. It has also started to happen in Russia, Brazil and some Eastern European countries.

With real contribution through knowledge power and cheaper labor managed by knowledge power, almost any 3rd world and developing countries can attract investors to invest, rather than obtaining the loan from the World Bank or IMF usually with strong unfavorable terms. Yes, investors will also take good part of the profit but that's normal. If with investor's money other countries can flourish, so can many other developing countries. The goal should be to continue to move up the food chain by continuing innovation and entrepreneurship. *Population should be considered as a real resource rather than as a social burden.*

Of course, some people would not be able to learn as much as others, go to school & get trained and educated (e.g. very poor people). For them also there is good news. They can be taught through ICT (Information and communication technology) and Internet to do something better than what they are doing now.

The basic idea is to **educate and transform their (have-nots) brains into a huge resource.** One key goal here is to teach them what Internet is, how it can help them, especially how they can do some business with the Internet (e.g. they can create some important portals, blogs, courses etc) and teach others and make money. Or they can do an e-commerce portal, make ICT as part of many businesses, become smart in getting outsourced projects etc. In fact, we expect to see some good surprises from such population group once they learn how to use the Internet—this is because the Internet was mainly designed for literate people. So, the Internet applications and its usage today reflect the behaviors of the literate people. Once illiterate people learn and start using the Internet, various new types of applications will be developed to meet the needs of such population group resulting in many new types of applications and businesses.

Education needs to be reformed to meet local, regional and global needs. Education needs to be practical, focused and goal oriented, like driving the economy. Thus, there needs to be emphasis on innovation and entrepreneurship. Educational reform should focus on both short term and long term needs. It should also focus on both formal and informal (like vocational institutes, training centers of various types) education. Almost all countries have education as their top priority and planning to make sure that everyone can get an education. However, extending education to everyone using conventional means may be difficult and impractical. For example, many rural areas in many developing countries do not have schools. Building schools covering all such areas would be expensive and may take a long time. A quicker way to provide education in such areas would be through e-Learning or distance learning, especially with Voice Internet as many people living in such areas have some type of phone access but very limited computer access. This can further be enhanced by establishing Internet Café's when possible.

In this endeavor, many organizations including Governments, NGOs, UN, Foundations, Research Institutions, Corporations, Service providers, Civil Societies and others would need to work together. Many corporations (for example, CISCO, Microsoft, Intel, IBM and Google) have various philanthropic programs to help bridge the Digital Divide. Inclusion of Voice Internet and Voice Computer in these programs would help expedite the bridging process. There are various other organizations (for example Social Business based companies) who are closely working to help bridge the Digital Divide as a part of their core business. Various other companies have core businesses to help the poor and eradicate poverty. A good example is Grameen Bank and micro-credit inspired businesses. As the Nobel Laureate Dr. Muhammad Yunus, the founder of the Grameen Bank concept, well stated in his 2006 Nobel Lecture, "Poverty is the absence of all human rights. The frustrations, hostility and anger generated by abject poverty cannot sustain peace in any society. For building stable peace we must find ways to provide opportunities for people to live decent lives." Thus, it is a natural choice and also very important to work together with all such organizations and companies to achieve our goal to minimize gaps between the have and have-nots.

What can we expect after truly bridging the Digital and Language Divides, reforming education with focus on innovation and entrepreneurship, providing such education to many people who are on the side on "have-nots", and then nurturing their education through good practical business model? Well, it should create a **huge very useful skilled force (resource)** that can not only help improve their own economy (i.e. transforming the **"Digital Divide" into "Digital Opportunity"**) but also help improve the world economy. In fact, it will also help various other global developments including social, cultural and political. Many new companies, products & services will emerge that will be sold globally. The rich will also use newly developed highly skilled brains of the poor to get even richer by investing in this vast human resource. As a result **money will start flowing from rich to poor in a substantial way naturally which is essential to really minimize rich-poor gap, eradicate poverty and achieve other MDGs.** Circulating money mainly within the poor people through various existing methods (e.g. Social Businesses) is great and should be continued and expanded without any doubt. But to minimize the rich-poor gap and for poor to become part of the main stream economic system, money has to flow from rich to poor in a substantial way; and that is possible via valuable resource creation from the bottom of the pyramid people.

This huge resource will also grow fast, for various reasons; the two key reasons are:

(a) firstly, their (have-not's) brains are as good as many good brains on the "have" side. They (have-nots) may be poor from financial standpoint but not from intelligence standpoint.
(b) Secondly, bridging the Digital Divide would provide these people more freedom, better economy and social status. More freedom

will in turn make them more innovative. As Nobel Laureate Dr. Amartya Sen [Sen1999] well stated ". . . . more freedom results in more rationality which in turn results more innovation . . ." A practical simple example is designing applications for the poor. Today, most companies focus their products/services on 10%-15% population in the top of the pyramid as they can pay a higher price resulting good Gross Margin and profitability. Very few companies are designing products / applications for the "poor". Once bottom of the pyramid people learn innovation and entrepreneurship, they would be the real contributors to design for the poor as they would feel and understand their needs more than anyone else. And in fact, Voice Internet itself can help this design process as many on-line software applications and services can be readily designed for the poor; thus enabling them to create various new profitable businesses including on-line Banking For the Poor, on-line Trading/Transactions for the Poor, various products helping in Healthcare, Farming, Education, various mobile applications for the Poor and many more!

There are various other key added benefits—once base of the pyramid people get out of the poverty (and some become rich as well), all poverty related issues will be minimized or eliminated totally. Key poverty related issues are terrorism, spreading diseases, committing various social crimes, refugees from the developing world, disruption of law & order, not advancing education, healthcare, social depression and the like. Thus, by letting base of the Pyramid people get out of poverty will in turn greatly help achieve **global peace**.

Moreover, poor people would be able to participate in and help to reshape world economy. Of course we would need to set our expectations right. The already rich (both financially and brain-wise) people will keep on inventing new things and get richer and it might be difficult for the new comers to catch up or overcome them in many aspects. **But there is no limit to innovation. So, in turn, all will be benefited driving a new world of prosperity with much lower gap between rich and poor and with significantly increased world peace.**

Acknowledgements

This book is dedicated to my wife, Sayema, my daughters, Tonima and Tasnia, my son Tahsin and son-in-law, Ghalib for their loving support.

A good part of this book derives from my involvement with InternetSpeech, Inc which I had founded in 1999. I have had opportunities to interact with many customers, colleagues, investors, companies, governments, organizations, foundations, civil societies, news media, researchers, faculty members from various universities and individuals. I thank them all for their help in making my ideas more relevant to our existing and future potential users worldwide, especially at the Bottom of the Pyramid.

Special acknowledgements go to Dr. Craig Barret, former Chairman of GAID (United Nations Global Alliance for ICT) and Intel; Mr. Sarbuland Khan, former Executive Coordinator at GAID; Ms. Haiyan Qian, Director, UNDESA (U.N. Department of Economic and Social Affairs) and Dr. Abdul Waheed Khan, Director, UNESCO (United Nations Economic, Social and Cultural Organization), Prof. Geoffrey Lungwangwa, Minister of Communications and Transport, Zambia and Mr. Felix Mutati, Minister of Commerce, Trade and Industry, Zambia.

Special acknowledgements also go to Mr. Alan Capper from the South South News; Mr. David Kirk Patrick from the Fortune Magazine and Prof. Mohammad Yunus, 2006 Nobel Laureate in Peace. And, of course, special acknowledgements to all of my colleagues at InternetSpeech, Inc. And the same to my family.

Special acknowledgements also go to many of our customers and partners, especially, Mr. Sundeep Bedi, Founder and CEO of Knowaysys; Mr. Nitin Mohite, VP of Operations, Knowaysys; Mr. Isaiah Z. Chabala, former

Ambassador of Zambia to the United Nations and European Union; Mr. Tyson B. Chisambo from Visionary Consulting Associates, Inc; Mr. Arnab Sen, Founder & CEO of Flitser; Mr. Ravi Sankar and Mr. Vamsi Karatam from Samvi Software; Mr. Venkata Mallineni, VP, Sify Technologies; Mr. Vyas and Mr. Anand from Abt, India; Mr. Goyal, Managing Director, MTNL (Mahanagar Telephone Nigam Limited), Mumbai; Mr. Raja Srnivas, VP, Tata Tele Services; Dr. Rajan, former Managing Director, Tata Tele Services; Mr. MAS Reddy; General Manager, Business Development, BSNL(Bharat Sanchar Nigam Limited), Hyderabad; Mr. Shankar Aggarwal, Joint Secretary, Ministry of Communications and Information Technology, Government. of India; Dato' Wahab Abdullah, Managing Director, of MIMOS (*Malaysian* Institute Of Microelectronic Systems); Mr. Thilai Raj, VP, MIMOS; Mr. Nagen Perumal, Director, MIMOS; Mr. Kitipong Sutti, Director TAB (Thailand Association for the Blind); Mr. Torpong Selanon, VP, TAB; Senator Monthian Buntan, President of TAB; Dr. Pansak, Dr. Prakasit, and Ms. Wantanee from NECTEC (National Electronics and Computer Technology, Thailand); Mr. Wisit from ITU (International Telecommunication Union); Dr. Kim, Director, ITU, Dr. Xuan, Director, ESCAP (U.N. Economic and Social Commission for Asia and Pacific); Mr. Robert Faithful, Senior Policy Analyst, U.S. Dept. of Interior; Mr. Will Bauman, VP, Computer Associates; Larry McArthur, CEO, McArthur Associates; Mr. Larry Lewis, President & Founder, Flying Blind LLC; Mr. Jaroslaw Urbanski, Founder, Harpo (Poland); Mr. Larry Maggard, President, iWebTalk; S.M. Iqbal, Managing Director; ISN (Bangladesh); Mr. Nasir-ur Rahman Sinha, Chairman, ACME Group (Bangladesh); Mr. Iqbal Hussaiyn, Managing Director, Magnum Engineering & Construction Limited, Bangladesh; Mr. Enayetur Rahman, Managing Director, Ulka Semiconductor, Bangladesh; Mr. John Morton-Hicks from United Kingdom; Mr. Rafiq Hussain from Advanced Micro Devices; Mr. Yanagawa from Hitachi, Mr. Deepak Yadav, President at Swami Vivekanand Education Society; Mr. Vinod Malhotra, Managing Director, ICR India; Mr. Alex Lee, Managing Director, RA Consulting, China; Mr. Suprem Haron and Mr. Mahmud Jeludin from Radius Technology, Brunei; Ms. Kimberly Casey, InfoPoverty Foundation; Prof. Pierpaolo Saporito from OCAAM (Observatory for Cultural and Audiovisual Communication, an UNESCO created Agency to fight poverty) and Prof. Craig Smith, Founder of the Digital Divide Institute.

The following organizations and Foundations deserve special acknowledgements—NFB (National Foundations of the Blind), ACB (American Council of the Blind), AFB (American Foundations of the Blind), CNIB (Canadian Foundations of the Blind), TAB (Thailand Association for the Blind), AARP (American Association of the Retired People), ASA (American Society on Aging), International Lighthouse, San Francisco Lighthouse, Miami Lighthouse, Lions Club, U.N. GAID (United Nations Global Alliance for ICT), ITU (International Telecommunication Union), OCCAM (Observatory for Cultural and Audiovisual Communication, an UNESCO created Agency to fight poverty), WFIS (World Forum on Information Society) and the Digital Divide Institute.

Finally, special thanks and appreciation to the Founding President of Zambia, Dr. Kenneth David Kaunda for his generous and touching Foreword for this book.

My sincere apology for many people who helped but I could not mention their names here.

Emdad Khan, March 2011, California, U.S.A

About the Book

The "Internet for Everyone: Reshaping the Global Economy by Bridging the Digital Divide" presents a practical, very affordable, easy to learn and use method to enjoy the benefits of the Internet using any phone and user's voice. It discusses the existing approaches of bridging the Digital Divide and shows why existing approaches alone will not be able to really bridge the Digital Divide.

The book introduces the concept of the Language Divide, and emphasizes that it is equally important to bridge the language divide so that non-English speaking people can equally access the most of the content of the Internet which is currently dominated in English. It presents a new technology called **Voice Internet** that allows anyone to access the Internet using any phone and user's voice, and shows how Voice Internet can really help bridge the Digital and Language Divides globally, by eliminating most of the difficulties (e.g. un-affordability, difficulty to use and learn, need for literacy, difficulty in viewing on small screen, difficulty in using small keypad, difficulty in navigation and the like) associated with the existing visual driven approaches using computers, personal devices, high end and medium end Internet enabled phones.

The book emphasizes that Voice Internet technology rides on existing infrastructure (e.g. existing telecom or wireless networks), existing websites (e.g. over 3 billion websites from the World Wide Web), existing distribution networks (e.g. telecom providers, mobile telephone providers. Internet Service Providers and Application Service Providers), and thus shows how deployment and adoptability is faster and easier.

Providing access to the Internet or information is the first step. But there are various other key steps to exploit the real benefits of the Information

Age. Three such major key steps are Education, Innovation and Entrepreneurship. These in, turn, can help in Economic, Social, Cultural, Political and other developments, especially, of the Bottom of the Pyramid people (BOP). The book discusses in details how the BOP can really use Voice Internet and related products and services to become an enormous resource not just for themselves but also for the top of the pyramid (rich people) in the world. Examples are included for improved farming, education, health, getting jobs and creating jobs. The book emphasizes that to really help minimize the rich-poor gap (and also achieve other Millennium Development Goals (MDGs) of the United Nations), a significant amount of money would need to flow from the rich to the poor. The existing methods do not seem to achieve that as already proven by the fact that the rich-poor gap has been increasing consistently for a long time.

To ensure significant money flow from rich to the poor in a natural and sustainable way, as already mentioned, the book put emphasis on creating an enormous resource from the BOP by using affordable Internet Access. Education, Entrepreneurship, Innovation and use of a good Business Model are essential to ensure sustainability with good growth. Use of such an enormous resource will cause significant of money to flow from rich to the poor in three broad ways:

- Rich will use the low cost enormous resource (e.g. through outsourcing)
- BOP will start developing various new products and services (especially suitable for the bottom 90% of people), many of which would also be attractive to the rich people
- BOP will import much less products and services form the rich.

This will also help more money to circulate within the BOP.

Thus, many from BOP would become richer and the rich-poor gap would be minimized significantly worldwide.

The funding needs of the BOP to start businesses will come from various existing funding sources including the already very successful Microfinance lenders as Voice Internet will help entrepreneurs to do new things with less competition, increased revenue and with a higher margin; thus generating more for the lenders and the borrowers, resulting in an attractive win-win relationship.

This book is good for decision makers / policy makers at the Governments, Organizations, Foundations, Corporations, Civil Societies, educators, students, entrepreneurs, innovators and also the rich individuals, especially, those who would like to help many BOP around the world.

Author's Biography

Dr. Emdad Khan is president and CEO of InternetSpeech. He founded the company in 1998 with the vision to develop innovative technology for accessing information on the Internet anytime, anywhere, using just an ordinary telephone and the human voice.

As a pioneer in the Internet voice space, Khan is a frequent speaker at voice-recognition, Internet applications, bridging the Digital & Language Divides, Global Economic Development and other industry, academia & organization trade shows and conferences. He holds 22 patents and has published numerous papers on the advent of voice technology on the Internet, neural networks, fuzzy logic, intelligent systems, VLSI (Very Large Scale Integration) and optics. Khan's acute technical knowledge and keen understanding of emerging markets has played an important role in the development of InternetSpeech's first product/service netECHO®, the only product available today that delivers complete access to the Internet using voice.

Voice Internet is deployed by various service providers & organizations, and many users around the world are using Voice Internet to access the Internet by talking and listening using any phone.

During his career, Khan invented, defined, developed and deployed worldwide new intelligent software products for micro-controller-based home appliances. He has also created and deployed speech recognition based Internet applications. He has 20 years of experience with large semi-conductor companies, including Intel and National Semiconductor.

Khan is still doing active research. His current major interest is to use brain-like and brain-inspired algorithms to solve some open problems, especially, NLU (Natural Language Understanding) which is very well aligned for InternetSpeech's next generation products & services to allow users (especially bottom of the pyramid people) to interact with the Internet using their natural language.

Khan was born in Bangladesh. He worked at Bangladesh University of Engineering & Technology as a faculty before emigrating to US. He has also taught courses at other universities and industry conferences on VLSI, neural networks, fuzzy logic and Intelligent Agent. He holds a doctorate in computer science, master of science degrees in electrical engineering and engineering management, and a bachelor of science degree in electrical engineering.

Emdad Khan currently lives with his family in the San Francisco Bay Area in California.

PART ONE

The World
of Divides and Gaps

Chapter 1

A Quick Look at Today's World

In this world of over 6.5 billion people, over 4 billion people are poor—40% live in poverty, and 16% live in extreme poverty. The World Bank defines poverty as living on less than $2 a day, absolute or extreme poverty as living on less than $1 a day. Nobel Laureate Joseph Stiglitz in his fascinating latest book "Making Globalization Work[1]" says "Think for a minute what it means to live on one or two dollars a day. Life for people this poor is brutal. Childhood malnutrition is endemic, life expectancy is often below fifty years, and medical care is scarce. Hours are spent each day searching for fuel and drinkable water and . . . .". Apart from inadequate income, two other issues are heavily associated with people living below the poverty line: insecurity and powerlessness. One World Bank report published a nice statement from a young poor woman in Jamaica that captures the sense of powerlessness: "Poverty is like living in jail, living under bondage, waiting to be free". In general, poor have few opportunities to speak out. When they speak, no one listens; when someone does listen, the reply is that nothing can be done; when they are told something can be done, nothing is ever done.

On the other side of the coin there are the rich people, much smaller in number, but they own over 80% of the world wealth!!! They enjoy all the benefits of the civilization, they control the world economy, they control world business, world laws—they control almost everything except poverty. Well, not quite true though. They try to minimize poverty by donation, philanthropy, foundations etc. Obviously that is not enough since the poverty has been increasing for a long time now.

In 2004, the United Nations took a new initiative to minimize poverty and improve the equity distribution in this unfair world. This is called the Millennium Development Goals. [LinkMDG] We will take a look at that shortly. But before that, let's take a closure look at this enormous gap between rich and poor; what are the causes, what are the types of gaps, are there other similar gaps, can these gaps be bridged, if so how and the like.

Broadly speaking, the inequality is inherent in mother-nature. The natural resources of the world were not uniformly distributed when the world was created, different races were born in different parts of the world getting different resources, not every human is born with same capabilities, not every human develops the same level of intelligence even under the "same" environment etc etc. In short, by birth we are all different; the equity is different to begin with. So, as we grew as a human race, more gaps and inequities got developed. Today, we have rich-poor gap, gap in natural resources, gap in ethnicity, gap in male-female capabilities, gap due to the computer revolution (The so called Digital Divide), the gap due to disabilities and so on. Even a much simpler gap can be seen through students in a class. Assume that a class has all the good equipments—like a computer for each student, a nice projector so that everyone could easily see the lecture notes and everyone could hear the teacher very well. However, not all students in such a class will perform equally. This implies that even if we do our best to minimize all the gaps, because of its inherent property some gaps will remain. That is why Darwin said "only the fittest will survive".

Should we try to reduce all these gaps? Can we really make these gaps go away? If so, how can we do so? These are the few key issues we will discuss throughout this book. Our premise is that the gap is an inherent property in this world. So, not all gaps can be eliminated or reduced to the same degree. For example, natural resources—a country cannot just acquire its missing natural resources. We have some good control on some gaps and relatively less control on other gaps. The Digital Divide, for example, is a gap that can be reduced to a good level when we compare it to reducing the gap between the rich and poor. Yes, bridging the Digital Divide, will eventually help reduce the gap between the rich and poor but there are many other factors that contribute to the rich-poor gap.

In general we should try to minimize all the gaps—no questions about that. But we would need to set our expectation right—that there will be some gaps no matter how well we try to minimize them as gap is inherent in the system. **However, by lowering gaps to a good level and keep on lowering will continue to yield a better world and hence that should be our goal.**

Many organizations, foundations, civil societies, and individuals have been trying to minimize these gaps. One such key organization is the United Nations (UN)—in 2004, the UN took a new initiative to minimize poverty and improve the global distribution of wealth. This is called the Millennium Development Goals [LinkMDG]. Many people are working together to achieve this worthwhile global dream by 2015. These MDGs are

- End Poverty & Hunger
- Provide Universal Education
- Ensure Gender Equality
- Good Child Health
- Good Maternal Health
- Combat HIV/AIDS
- Ensure Environmental Sustainability
- Ensure Global Partnership

Many people around the world have written extraordinary papers, books, and reports on rich-poor gaps, poverty reduction, globalization, bridging the Digital Divide and many related topics. One such book is—"Making Globalization Work" by Nobel Laureate Joseph Stiglitz. Stiglitz very nicely pointed out the key issues with globalization and how such issues can be addressed to make globalizations work worldwide for both poor and rich to ensure minimizing some of the key gaps mentioned above. Another good book is "Creating a World Without Poverty" by Nobel Laureate Muhammad Yunus [Yunus2007]. Yunus proposed a new approach called "Social Business" where the key objective of the business is to provide social benefits rather than the traditional objective of profit maximization.

Another good book is "Out of Poverty" by Paul Polak [Polak2008]. Paul provides a very good description of how to get out of poverty using some very successful examples. "The Fortune at The Bottom of the Pyramid: Eradicating Poverty through Profits" by C.K Prahlad [Prahlad2004] and "How to Change the World: Social Entrepreneurs and the Power of the New Ideas" by David Bornstein [Bornstein 2005] are two other good books.

Stiglitz has pointed out that in spite of so much works done by so many organizations (including the World Bank and IMF—International Monetary Fund), poverty has been increasing rather than decreasing. The key reasons are:

a) Organizations (including corporations) involved in this process try to solve it but without really giving up their key goals like high profitability and having good financial control. Associated policies actually helped lenders much more and borrowers much less.

b) Because of (a), many governments took loan with unfavorable terms and paying high interest; thus forcing them to spend less on the development. It has caused a big "debt burden" for many countries. It has also contributed to the global financial instability.

c) The need for "reserve" for each country (indirectly came from the Global financial system), caused money to actually flow from poor to the rich (instead of the other way around)—for example US is borrowing (or developing and poor countries are lending) $2B per day (this figure is lowered to some extent after the financial melt-down during end of 2008) by selling its T-Bill with a very low interest rate. If this money could be lent at higher interest rate or not lend at all, each country could spent the same for key development. This has resulted in an unstable Global Reserve system.

d) Economic globalization has outpaced political globalization.

e) Globalization without good Global rule.

Stiglitz recommendations include

1. A new World Financial Reserve System that help money flow from rich to poor.

2. Democratization of Globalization.
3. Strengthening political globalization to make it comparable to economic globalization.
4. Making the trade fair between rich and poor countries.
5. A good and stable way to eliminate the burden of debt.
6. Improving corporate role for social responsibility, less cost for poor countries, less profit from poor countries, limiting the power of corporations, improving corporate governance, and reducing the scope of corruption.

Such suggested policies, recommendations and plans are very good. However, as Stiglitz points out, implementation of these proposed solutions would be difficult mainly because the stake holders would not really give up their key goals like high profitability and having good financial control whereas the suggested recommendations do not encourage high profitability and high financial control for valid reasons.

Even though these might be difficult to implement, these are undoubtedly good goals. However, these are at very high level. To really minimize all gaps, we would need more specifics, especially complementary recommendations at implementation level so that we can achieve the desired goals. In fact, for some of the key problems, we would need to look at from the **bottom-up**. A good example is converting the base of the pyramid people (mainly poor people) into a **huge resource rather than keeping them as a social burden** by involving them as part of the solution rather than as part of the problem. Paul has shown some good examples to get out of poverty by increasing daily earnings from $1 a day to several dollars a day. His key suggestions are:

a) to understand the root cause of poverty (especially extreme poverty i.e. people living with less than a $1 per day income) by directly talking to the poor people to clearly understand their problems and root cause, and then developing appropriate and affordable solutions for their problems so that they can earn more through their own existing efforts. For example, for farmers, the key issue was to do more in production as well as in sale so that their earning was enough to get out of poverty. The root problem in this regard was lack of a low cost irrigation tool. Paul and IDE (International Development Enterprise with Paul as one of the Founders [LinkIDE]) had worked together to fund and provide a good solution to the irrigation problem and helped millions of people to get out of poverty. Such solutions also include developing and marketing technologies for water access and control, providing expertise and training, and increasing access to markets.

b) To identify new related products to generate new revenue with minimal efforts. In this regard one example is that Paul & IDE helped people to plant new fruit trees and use that to generate new revenues.

Paul has also made several other very good suggestions including "designing for the other 90%" (traditional design focus on the rich 10% customers whereas a low cost affordable design can provide a profitable solutions to a much larger 90% market) and how other organizations can help people to get out of poverty and prosper.

C.K. Prahlad has outlined how fortune can be made from the bottom of the Pyramid people by showing several examples using successful projects in various parts of the world. He highlighted the ways that enterprises can follow to deliver products & services to the developing world in a manner that help developing world to prosper while at the same time enterprises can make fortune from poor people in the developing world.

C.K. Prahlad's ideas are very good and some corporations have started focusing on those. However, today's corporations mainly focus on the top 10% people as Paul mentioned in his book. Changing this for many major corporations to focus on the remaining 90% people will be difficult and will take a long time. Designing for the top 10% and doing business with them has a different paradigm than doing business with the bottom 90% who cannot easily afford to buy, return on investment (ROI) from whom would not be high and the like. However, once a good number of corporations show the way successfully, this trend will change and many corporations will adopt and focus on doing business with bottom 90%.

Yunus has shown how microcredit can help many **extremely poor** people from the bottom of the pyramid to get out of poverty. Yunus has also shown great social benefits through various Social Businesses.

The recommendations made by Paul Polak, C.K Prahlad, Mohammad Yunus and many others are very good recommendations to get out of poverty and should be continued and enhanced when possible. But to do even better, especially, for the extremely poor (to not just get out of poverty but to be more successful financially), we will need to do more, and that is the main focus of this book. The **recommendations made in this book are applicable for extremely poor, poor, middle class and to some extent for rich people**. By "truly" Bridging the Digital Divide, we can enable such people to focus on education; and by going beyond bridging the Digital Divide, these people can focus **on entrepreneurship and innovation** resulting in real economic, social and other developments for themselves (i.e. transforming the **"Digital Divide" into "Digital Opportunity"**), and a huge low cost resource for the rest of the world.

This will also indirectly help some of the issues mentioned in Stiglitz's book. For example, it will help the global reserve system. Why? Well, if we analyze carefully, the real reason, countries are buying T-Bills mainly from US, in spite of such a high cost, is to ensure that their economy is less volatile—providing higher confidence to others to do business and trade with them. But then why mainly US T-Bill? Because as a country and its currency, the US is very stable that one can really depend on (this is changing to some extent because of the recent financial melt-down but many still believe that US will come out of such a down-turn soon). And the real reason for US stability is because of its **high sustained innovation and entrepreneurship for a long time.** *The same can be true (at least to a good extent) if a poor or developing country can really start doing innovation and entrepreneurship, and make & sell new products/services globally. When this happens, the need to keep high "reserve" will be minimized and other countries will have much more confidence in any country really creating and selling new products and services worldwide.*

"Truly" Bridging the Digital Divide will also extend some of the ideas that Polak, Prahlad, and others have mentioned. For example, helping the people in slums with the benefits of the Internet, entrepreneurship and innovation will enable them to do much more in increasing their income and society's income.

We will limit the scope of this book to the issues with the **Digital Divide and Language Divide ONLY** and their impact on other gaps including

how bridging the Digital Divide can really change the World economy, but we are not going to specifically address issues related to how to bridge other gaps, although bridging the Digital Divide will help bridge many other gaps including the rich-poor gap.

The Digital Divide

The **digital divide** is the gap between those with regular, effective access to digital technologies and those without. In other words, those who are able to use technology for their own benefit and those who can not. Major digital technologies are the computer, Internet, PDA (Personal Digital Assistance) and smart cell phones. "Effective Access" has two broad forms—(a) availability of a digital device and (b) learning how to use a digital technology.

Our society has changed significantly since the advent of the computer. Computing power has changed how we do business, how we communicate, how we store information and how we compute, just to name a few. Like any new technology, computers were very expensive initially and only businesses and some Governments could afford to buy them. When the Personal computer was introduced in early 1980, the price became within reach of many consumers. However, the number of such consumers who could afford to buy a computer was still much lower than those who could not afford to buy one. This gap due to the computer revolution is called the Digital Divide. This divide, however, started shortening as the price of computers continued to fall.

It is important to note that as the number of computers grew, connecting them with a network became more and more important.

Also, the amount of information connected to computers continued to grow rapidly. These two key factors resulted in the largest source of Information, the Internet. Unfortunately, many people who had computers could not get an easy connection to the Internet and were left unconnected. This caused the gap to widen between those who could more effectively use the benefits of the information than those who could not. This gap somewhat further divided the world and widened the Digital Divide caused by not having computers.

Another key part of the Digital Divide is the difficulty in learning how to use a computer. Many people find learning how to use a computer difficult. This is mainly true for the elderly people, blind & visually impaired people, and dyslexic people. The continuous change in application software, Windows and other operating systems, new software, virus, spyware, adware, new features like podcast, multimedia, blogs, complex form filling and the like make it difficult for many people to learn (or keep on learning) these (and other new technologies) and be comfortable with these.

Yet another part of the Digital Divide is "artificial Digital Divide" which means that a person has a computer, and knows how to use it but cannot really use it because of the environment—e.g. while driving or moving in a position where eyes and hands are both busy.

Apart from the Digital Divide caused by computers and Internet, other devices also contributed to the Digital Divide, although to a much less extent. In general, any new technology causes some Divide. PDA, for example, caused some Divide as for many people learning how to use PDA do not find it easy. Cell phones, on the other hand, did not cause much Divide because anyone could at least easily learn how to make a phone call with a cell phone. However, many people do not know how to use all the other features like text messaging, setting alarms, downloading ring tones and the like. TV and TV remote control also did not cause much Divide as most people can easily learn the basic functions of such devices.

In this technology dominated world, on the one hand we are advancing at a fast rate as new technologies are invented. But on the other hand many people have difficulty coping up with such fast technological changes; thus creating even more gaps between who have and who don't have, and who can and who can't easily learn.

It is clear that the Digital Divide is actually widening considering all possible aspects—yes, for some aspects the Divide is getting minimized, e.g. gaps between some developing countries and rich countries; but for most aspects, the Divide is growing, especially between the Bottom of the Pyramid people and the rich people (More on this in the next few Sections).

Dimensions of the divide

The digital divide is not a clear single gap that divides a society into two groups as briefly described above. Digital Divide rather has multiple dimensions, some of which are implied above.

The first dimension of the Digital Divide is **having** or **not having a computer** or a personal device like PDA (Personal Digital Assistance). The second dimension is the difficulty in **learning** how to use a computer. Many people get intimidated with computers to begin with. Many start learning with good enthusiasm and courage but then find it difficult to learn or use.

The third dimension is the **connectivity** issue—not all computers are connected to the Internet. Connectivity, an important part of ICT (information and Communication Technology) is key to connect a computer (or similar devices) to the Internet. Physical connectivity is achieved mainly using wire line, wireless and satellite. Such major connectivity methods can use Dial-up, Broadband and other connection mechanism to connect to the Internet. These days, without an Internet connection, the use of a computer becomes very limited. Also, for many countries (especially developing countries) a power supply is not available which severely limits the use of computers as battery based usage is very limited.

Another dimension of the Digital Divide includes such forms as lower-performance computers, lower-quality or high-priced connections (i.e. narrowband or dialup connections), and difficulty in obtaining the Internet and technological advances in developing economies. Many people can get low cost access in local Internet Cafes, but the evidence still suggest that people are much more likely to make regular use of an Internet connection at home than anywhere else [LinkORBICOM].

Another key dimension of the Digital Divide is the global digital divide, reflecting existing economic divisions in the world. This global digital divide widens the gap in economic divisions around the world. Countries with a wide availability of Internet access can advance the economics of that country on a local and global scale. In today's society, jobs and education are directly related to the internet. In countries where the internet and other technologies are not accessible, education is suffering, and uneducated people cannot compete in our global economy. This leads to poor countries suffering greater economic downfall and richer countries advancing their education and economy.

Literacy contributes to another dimension—at least at the current stage of digital technology, the Internet is effectively **unusable by people who cannot read**, and is all but unusable if one doesn't know one or more of the primary languages of the Internet. Hence literacy presents a problem at several levels.

Yet another dimension is the unavailability of needed **content**. The Internet is very rich with various content but people in many countries do not have the knowledge or capabilities to create or put content relevant to them on the internet.

Social and Legal Constraints, including censorship and denial of access creates another dimension: there are a number of countries, including some very populous ones, who attempt to strictly control access to the Internet and to Internet resources.

Choice is another dimension—even if every other problem is resolved, there will be some people who will choose not to use the Internet, much as some people refuse to use the telephone, drive a car, or watch television.

And finally there is another key dimension, **Language Divide**—in fact this is another gap, of similar magnitude to the Digital Divide. Today, over 70% of the Internet content is in English. So, people in non English speaking countries cannot really use today's Internet, and hence are left out from the majority of Internet content. This gap is called the "**Language Divide**" which is addressed in Chapter 5.

Magnitude of the Digital Divide ([Sciadas2002], [Sciadas 2003]):

Describing the magnitude of the Digital Divide is not straightforward because the magnitude varies with almost each dimension mentioned above. In fact, there is no precise measure of the Digital Divide[7]. Given the complexity and the interdisciplinary nature of the problem, it has been difficult to establish a set of parameters that include the major issues affecting the characteristics and evolution of the Digital Divide. The evolution of the Digital Divide since its inception has **4 major Waves**:

First wave—provide computers and Internet access. This, although initially thought would bridge the major part of the Digital Divide, actually did not help as expected. It was discovered that not many people (especially in developing countries) were excited to learn and use a computer, to learn and use the Internet. It was realized that some specific applications would probably make people who are new to the Internet more interested.

Second wave—in this phase people were offered some specific applications solving some critical problems of interest. Associated training was considered and was supported by financial, academic and equipment & infrastructure providers. This phase helped in understanding the **inclusion of the socioeconomic** aspect. Although some isolated successful experiences were witnessed, the gap of the Digital Divide was not reduced noticeably.

Third wave—efforts of bridging the Digital Divide evolved to its 3rd phase that included key components of **grass root participation**, community leadership and sustainability related issues. The connection between technology and human development contributed to a better understanding of the Digital Divide. In many parts of the world several communities have experienced the benefits of the third wave and have been able to integrate first, second and third waves in search of higher levels of community prosperity.

Fourth wave—in this phase socioeconomic development with human values have strongly considered and significant use of successful Internet usage discovered (e.g. social networks).

Different parts of the world have different phases. Some parts have not even reached to third or fourth wave. In addition to the evolution of the Digital Divide, the Internet itself also evolved. Web2.0 contributed heavily in engaging many people from socioeconomic angle, mainly because of the structure letting people to interact much better with the Internet. The

ICT itself also evolved from dialup to broadband that has several versions including DSL, Wireless Broadband, Wi-Fi, Wi-Max, broadband over Power-line and Satellite. A good description on the ICT aspect of the Digital Divide can be found in [G@idICT2007].

"It is clear that the Digital Divide is not only a technology issue but also a human development issue. In order to reduce the gap it is necessary to acquire a new and more comprehensive vision of Sustainable Development that includes both the moral and intellectual leadership of the individual and the community" as mentioned in [Bracey2005].

Clearly, as already stated above, describing the magnitude of the Digital Divide is not straightforward. However, just to quantify the magnitude in some basic way, I have put a short description below. Obviously it does not reflect the magnitude of the real gap or Divide but it does tell some reasonable facts about the magnitude of the Divide. It also tells us whether the magnitude is really narrowing or widening.

In describing the magnitude of the Digital Divide and how the magnitude is evolving in a meaningful way, two good sources are [Sciadas2002] & [LinkORBICOM], both by Orbicom in collaboration with UNESCO, published in 2005 and 2004. The data in these sources are a bit old (1996-2003) but some recent (2009) data (later in this Chapter) show that the overall findings remained fairly valid till today. They have introduced some nice concepts like Infodensity (that includes ICT infrastructure and ICT skills), Info-use (ICT Uptake and ICT Intensity of use) and Infostate which is the combination of Infodensity and Info-use. They found that in 2003, the magnitude of the Digital Divide was huge—with an average country with a Infostate value of 100, the highest value (rich countries) was 231 while the lowest value (poor countries) was 5. Their findings also state that all the dimensions of the Digital Divide mentioned above contributed to the huge Divide with networking (connectivity) and skill the two big contributors. ***Commenting on "how the Digital Divide is evolving", it reported, "painfully slow pace. All things equal, it will take generations for countries at the bottom to achieve today's Infostate levels of countries in the middle . . . .".*** It also reported that networking grew significantly for many countries and regions between 1996 and 2003 (and beyond).

Skills and info-usage also grew significantly. *Yet, the overall Divide did not narrowed, it rather widened.*

Other organizations are also committed to monitor, track and help bridge the Digital Divide. One such example is the partnership between UNCTAD and ITU (the International Telecommunication Union)—UNCTAD and ITU have agreed to collaborate in their efforts to measure the magnitude of the digital divide and track global progress in the use of ICTs for development. With their combined expertise in developing indices and collecting statistics, the two organizations will provide an invaluable contribution to developing a Digital Opportunity Index (DOI), or composite ICT development index for international ICT performance evaluation and benchmarking.

The development of such an index is one of the goals of the Plan of Action adopted by the first phase of the World Summit on the Information Society (WSIS) [LinkWSIS], held in Geneva in December 2003. During the second phase of the Summit, which took place in Tunis, the DOI was launched. As noted in paragraph 115 of the Tunis Agenda for the Information Society, the DOI is part of an agreed methodology for monitoring progress in bridging the Digital Divide.

The International Telecommunications Union (ITU) just published "Measuring the Information Society" (2009) an ICT Development Index covering the period from 2002 to 2007. At first sight the top level figures appear encouraging: over 4 billion cell phone subscribers, 1.3 billion land lines, and almost 1.5 billion using the Internet. But what progress has been made over the past 5 years? Are more people in the developing world using the Internet? The conclusion of the report is *that "the magnitude of the digital divide is almost the same as five years before".*

Thus, it is very clear that **existing approaches have some key limitations as** otherwise the Digital Divide would have been narrowed during the last decade as opposed to getting widened during the same time period. Let's take a closure look at the existing approaches to bridge the Digital Divide.

Existing Approaches and their Limitations to Bridge the Digital Divide

Key existing approaches are

(a) provide low cost simple computers
(b) use TV with set top box
(c) use PDA
(d) use cell phone with some limited capability

For (a), sometimes limited computer training is also provided. All these are good approaches and these should be enhanced and continued. However, these approaches have many limitations.

For example, there are over 5 billion phones (as of this writing) worldwide [LinkCBSNews] as opposed to about 550 million connected computers. Thus, computers represent about 14% of the phone population. It is estimated that about a bit over 1.5 billion people (out of the 6.8 billion people in the world) have some sort of access to the Internet including the people using the Internet Café, Kiosks and the like [LinkInternetWorldStats]. Providing some type of computers to much more people in the world, especially, people at the bottom of the pyramid would take a very long time (a good example is electricity—after 100 years of invention of electricity, about 25% people in today's world do not yet have electricity [LinkGlobalIssues]). Besides, for many people (e.g. less educated or illiterate) learning how to use a computer is difficult. For many people (e.g. elderly, disabled), using a computer is challenging; many people who know how to use a computer find learning Internet very hard because of the difficult navigation, complex form filling, dealing with networking issues and the like; and many people who already know how to use a computer & Internet and do not have difficulty in using it, it is difficult for them to keep on learning new technologies that comes almost every day including pop-ups, memory clean alert, registry cure/ edits, adware, spyware and the like.

The alternate sources of computing and accessing the Internet are mainly personal devices like cell phone with good size display screen & with Internet capability, and Electronic devices like PDA (Personal

Development Assistance), and small computers (like Simputers). Such devices have been trying to make the Internet available to many more people. However, these devices also have many limitations like difficult user interface because of the small screen and small keypad, require to re-write the Internet content using another language (like WML—wireless markup language), several steps needed to navigate to desired content, not usable in an eyes busy—hand busy situation, the need for the users to know how to read and write and relatively high cost for many people. As a result, success of these devices in reducing the Digital Divide gap has been very limited. In fact, for some people learning how to use such simpler devices is difficult (even thought, in general, learning how to use such devices is easier compared to how to learn to use a computer), and many still cannot afford such devices, thus causing a wider Digital Divide.

So, a few obvious questions are:

(a) How can we really bridge the Divide or narrow the gap?
(b) How can we transform the Digital Divide into Digital Opportunity?
(c) How fast can we do it?
(d) How much existing approaches may contribute?
(e) Can a developing or poor country afford to bridge the gap using existing approaches?
(f) Will bridging the gap using existing technologies and methodologies be cost effective and provide good return on investment to the bottom of the pyramid people?

These are some of the key questions I will answer in this book. I will show that existing approaches to bridging the Digital and Language Divides are important but not sufficient to really bridge the Divides. In fact, **existing approaches alone will NOT be able to minimize or bridge** to an acceptable minimum level. I will show that other methods, especially, using **Phone and Voice based access** (called **Voice Internet**) are essential in bridging these Divides. Existing phone based approaches will not make it because of the un-addressed root problem of **"rendering"**, requirements to know how to read & write, to be literate to some extent (i.e. having some basic education about information and today's Internet), difficulty in learning computer interface (Operating System e.g. Windows), difficulty in learning Internet Interface (Browser e.g. Firefox), and cost. Although relatively new, the adoption of Voice Internet and associated technologies show strong promise to develop "Digital Aladdin's Lamp" (a simple device that would provide answers to most common questions asked verbally) that Yunus [Yunus2007] has envisioned.

I will also discuss what's next after successfully bridging the Digital and Language Divides. Especially, emphasizing on the fact that just bridging the Digital and Language Divides in its "raw" sense will help only to a limited extent. To really reap the benefits of bridging these divides, we would need to focus on **education, entrepreneurship and innovation** as these can really create resources, economic engines and convert the base of the pyramid people into a very valuable world resource. Once converted to a huge world resource, the base of the pyramid people can really help drive world economy as opposed to remain as social burden. They can actively and effectively drive **Economic, Social, Cultural** and other developments. **These people may be poor from "financial" standpoint but not from "intelligence" standpoint.** Money will flow from rich to poor because of the real value of the proposed huge **resource.** Such **money flow from rich to poor is essential to really minimize rich-poor gap, eradicate poverty and achieve other MDGs.** Circulating money mainly within the poor people through various existing methods (e.g. Social Businesses) is great and should be continued and expanded without any doubt. But to minimize the rich-poor gap and for poor to become part of the main stream economic system, money has to flow from rich to poor in a substantial way; and that is possible via valuable resource creation from the bottom of the pyramid people. We have already seen two such great successful examples—**China and India**. Resource creation will help this process of money flow from the rich to the poor in two broad ways:

(a) using the resources from the bottom of the pyramid by the rich e.g. via outsourcing.
(b) bottom of the pyramid people creating new products and services and selling to the rich.

Thus, successfully bridging the Digital & Language Divides by using proper ICT (information and communication technologies), and creating a huge resource from the bottom of the pyramid people by emphasizing on education, innovation and entrepreneurship, we can transform the Digital Divide into a great Digital Opportunity for the bottom of the pyramid people.

Voice Internet—A Practical Way to Bridge the Digital Divide & Help Create Digital Opportunity

Voice Internet technology allows anyone to access and enjoy the Internet using any phone and user's voice. Users basically make a phone call and an **automated attendant (Intelligent Agent)** allows the caller to access the Internet and enjoy surfing, searching, email, e-commerce and other features. Users basically **talk and listen to the Internet**. In other words, the telephone becomes the browser. An important feature of the Voice Internet is the **"rendering" feature that in real-time can convert any content from today's visually oriented websites into Short, Precise, Easily Navigable, and Meaningful** content that can be heard over any telephone (Core technology is from InternetSpeech, Inc *www. internetspeech.com*, a US based company). *This "rendering" feature is the key to allow any people to talk & listen to the Internet using any phone.*

Voice Internet overcomes all the above mentioned difficulties associated with existing devices like a computer, PDA or mobile phone in the following ways:

- no need to buy / use a computer which may be difficult for many people
- no need to buy a special device (thus allowing easy access to many more people)
- no need to deal with small screen or small keypad as users basically talk and listen
- much easier to learn as learning how to use a phone is much simpler than learning how to use a computer or personal device
- no need to re-write the content in another language. There are over 3 billion websites on the Internet. Re-writing all of them would cost over trillion dollars and hence not practical.
- No need for a person to know how to read or write as users basically talk and listen.

- No need for a person to know something about information and Today's Internet as Voice Internet automatically presents information from the Internet in a manner that most users are familiar with, e.g. presenting information as done in a radio broadcast or in a News Paper.
- Make it truly usable when mobile i.e. Enables one to use it in an Eyes Busy-Hands Busy situation
- And finally, much easier to learn and use the Internet as the **Intelligent Agent** eliminates the complex interface of an operating system and Internet browser, and make content retrieval, navigation, interaction and content upload very natural by solving the **rendering problem defined above.**

Thus, Voice Internet can provide the benefits of the Internet to **over 5 billion people** who have access to some type of phone; thus effectively **bridging the Digital Divide**. It also **bridges the Language** Divide as the "rendered content" can be translated in real time into another language. It is also an enabling technology to help create **Digital Opportunity** by allowing education, innovation and entrepreneurship to many people at the bottom of the pyramid. In fact, many users have been using Voice Internet since 2002. Voice Internet is described in details in Chapter 4.

Chapter 2

The need to Bridging The Digital Divide

The need to bridge the Digital Divide to help bottom of the Pyramid people to ensure social inclusion and improve their economic and other developments is probably obvious in a general sense. But it is important to take a deeper look to clearly understand the real implications and impacts.

As we all know we are in the Information Age and in this Information Age, "Information is Money" like "Time is Money". So, everyone should have the right to access any public information. The largest source of the information is the Internet. Accordingly, everyone in this world should have access to the Internet. Providing access to the Internet is a key component to bridge the Digital Divide. The other key components of the Digital Divide are having a computing device, learning how to use a computing device, learning how to use the Internet using a browser, and getting content in respective languages. Bridging the Digital Dive will help all the citizens of this world in many ways—as highlighted below:

1. Humanitarian ground / information for everyone
2. Economic development for the underdeveloped and developing countries
3. Neighbors must be good
4. Minimizing terrorism (ensure peace) through education and economic development
5. Increasing world productivity (underdeveloped and developing countries have many talents and untapped resources)

6. Health Improvement
7. Political, Social and cultural Developments
8. Minimizing corruption because of electronic processing etc
9. Increased innovation & entrepreneurship
10. Helping globalization
11. Use world knowledge for the benefit of mankind including the people at the bottom of the pyramid—they may be poor from financial standpoint but not from intelligence standpoint; thus it is possible to create a huge "human resource worldwide", especially from the bottom of the pyramid people
12. Helping "Design for the bottom 90%"
13. Ensuring Social Inclusion
14. Help minimizing the rich-poor gap
15. Ensuring Accessibility

Information for Everyone / Humanitarian ground:

Clearly, in this information age and information oriented society, information should be for everyone. Fortunately, this has already been established by United Nations effort in 2003 under the initiative called World Summit on Information Society (WSIS) [LinkWSIS]—
"We, the representatives of the peoples of the world, assembled in Geneva from 10-12 December 2003 for the first phase of the World Summit on the Information Society, declare our common desire and commitment to build a people-centered, inclusive and development-oriented Information Society, where everyone can create, access, utilize and share information and knowledge, enabling individuals, communities and peoples to achieve their full potential in promoting their sustainable development and improving their quality of life, premised on the purposes and principles of the Charter of the United Nations and respecting fully and upholding the Universal Declaration of Human Rights."

From a declaration standpoint, it is good as it came as a charter under the United Nations. However, how this will be truly accomplished, how effective it will be, how the effectiveness will be measured, and how this will be refined as needed are not clear. We all need to work together to ensure that this is really achieved in a practical way.

Economic development:

Economic development is very important for all countries, especially for the developing countries. Economic development without bridging the Digital Divide is becoming almost impossible. This is mainly because computer and information have become an integral part of economic development. People having computers and Internet access can make significant positive impact on almost all key factors that drive economy.

For example, access to information makes education, business processes, Government processes, manufacturing, farming—just to name a few—more efficient & effective. To have more uniform equity distribution, bridging the Digital Divide is very important not just for under developed and developing countries but also for the developed countries. Most developed countries still have high level Digital Divide in some races /groups (E.g. in US there is a large Divide for native Indians), Digital Divide in elderly people, Digital Divide in people with disabilities and the like.

Neighbors must be good:

We are living in a global world. In such a world, we must ensure that our neighbors are good so that we get all the benefits of having good neighborhood. In fact, having good neighborhood is becoming a necessity from safety standpoint. A good neighborhood can stimulate new ideas, cooperation and many other socio-economic-cultural initiatives that can help economic, social, cultural and other developments. To ensure that we have good neighbors, the "haves" should ensure that "have-nots" have access to all the key resources and benefits including good access to the Internet.

Minimize terrorism (ensure peace) through education and economic development:

One key way to minimize terrorism is education. Internet is a very good source of both formal and informal education. For people at the bottom of the pyramid, informal education is more important as many people would not be able to afford a formal education. Many people at the bottom of the pyramid do not know how to read or write. So, a formal education would not be even useful until illiteracy is removed first. Internet based informal education can be audio based (like podcast based learning) which does not need prior education. Besides, Internet can stimulate key informal education to such population groups—people can naturally talk, listen and learn. Education in turn will create values, help economic development (through productivity, new products or services and the like). People will be busy in learning via above mentioned activities, as it will help them in various ways, most importantly their economic condition. And hence they will be less interested in doing terrorist activities.

Increasing world productivity:

Globalization is happening fast and Internet is one of the key accelerators for globalization. Bridging the Digital Divide will help result in a skilled workforce around the world; thus, it will help productivity enhancement. In this dynamic information driven global economy, technology is key in developing many products & services, in the manufacturing process, in business, Government, NGO and other organization's business processes. Thus, skilled workforce is essential and the key to improve productivity.

For example, in a manufacturing environment (say garment industry, machine tools factory, or cell phone industry), if all the key information can be shared electronically (via a webpage or email), management and workers can communicate more effectively and hence can make their day to day work much more efficient by avoiding some face to face meetings or waiting to get a reply from the manager verbally. Managers and workers can also work in multi-modal environment—e.g. a manger can be in a meeting for a long time but can quickly send an important email to a colleague or customer without interrupting the meeting.

Productivity increase in many other setting are also very significant. For example, many Governments are already digitizing their key information so that such information can be be shared, modified and saved in a much more efficient way. People would not need to stay in a line for a long time to get an important Government form to fill as such a form can easily be downloaded from the website. Besides the form can be submitted electronically avoiding Government officer to record all data manually. In this case, it is not just productivity increase but also a huge saving in cost.

And if such forms can be filled verbally using any phone (e.g. registering for a new birth certificate or requesting for a job application), then much more people could participate in the process; thus making it much more useful, efficient and productive.

Health Improvement:

Much key health information is on the Internet. Patients can access such key information, communicate with doctors more easily, track medical history, get prescriptions and even buy medicine. Besides, many patients who may not have any medical insurance, can get lots of valuable information (e.g. about HIV, about Swine Flu and the like) from the Internet. Use of telemedicine is also growing and Internet access is an important element for that as well.

Political, Social and Cultural Development:

Political, social, cultural and similar other developments involve all types of people in the society. People from all levels of the society need to participate actively. Without bridging the Digital Divide, many people would not be able to participate in social, political and cultural activities. Internet is almost essential for socio-political-cultural advancement.
As an example, let's take election process in a country. Even though traditional radio, TV and other media provide a good coverage and people can interact and influence, share their views etc, use of Internet has become almost a necessity to do real-time feedback and tracking. During 2008 President Election in US, use of Internet was a major factor.

Minimizing corruption because of electronic processing:

Electronic processing will minimize the level of corruption at various levels including public and private sectors. All transactions and data will be recorded automatically and hence will force people not to cheat or bribe. Yes, some smart people may still like to manipulate in some ways and more intelligent software will evolve over time to minimize corruption led by such smart people. Overall result would be a significantly low level corruption, lowering cost, improving morality and productivity.

Increased innovation & entrepreneurship:

Innovation and entrepreneurship are the two key factors to drive "economic" engine and hence economic and social development. Educating all the people of the world is good and essential but NOT sufficient to drive economy. Without really bridging the Digital and Language Divide, innovation and entrepreneurship would be very slow and would not be effective in a meaningful way.

For example, the borrowers of Grameen Bank usually do business that meets local needs like buying cows and selling milk. Or they may buy daily necessity items like eggs, chickens and the like at a lower price from one village and sell those at a higher price. These days they use cell phone a lot in finding out related key information like where the price is lowest or what price the competition is selling at. **It is worth noting that before cell phone was not widely available, many village people came out of poverty by using the Village Phone program, through which women entrepreneurs started a business providing wireless payphone service in rural areas of Bangladesh. This is a good example that can easily be extended to the Internet, especially using Voice Internet access.** Thus, some village entrepreneurs can quickly learn how to use Voice Internet and then start teaching others how to access and use the Internet. Once such entrepreneurs teach Voice Internet to a sizeable population, they in turn can use the Internet to do other innovative businesses, improve their education, improve their health and much more. For example, **farmers can learn key information on farming, how to use right insect killers, how to improve their production and the like. They can also start selling directly to the buyer at a much higher price as the buyer would be able to bypass expensive middlemen.** *Automating this type of processes via Internet would not only make the process more efficient but also enable new entrepreneurial and innovative businesses.*

A good such example would be voice commerce using local language. Another example would be e-Learning. Some may quickly learn how to create blogs and how to upload content by voice using Voice Internet. A bit advanced people (having some education), would learn how to create websites and important applications as there would be instant users providing necessary incentives to sustain the process thru business. **The key idea is the fact that once we can make them learn and use the Internet in its easiest form and show them how to use that to help in their day to day activities, the real benefits of the Information Age will be readily extended to such un-served population.**

Help Globalization:

Globalization process needs information to be shared first to all the people, create resources at all possible places, use resources at all places, create infrastructure to distribute materials at all places and so on. Bridging the Digital and Language Divide are the keys to ensure maximum participation from all demography and all places in the world.

Use world knowledge for the benefits of mankind:

As mentioned above, bridging the Digital Divide in true sense will help education, entrepreneurship and innovation. This in turn will help economic and social development. But it can also create a huge human resource worldwide by properly manipulating key advantages of education, entrepreneurship and innovation. The bottom of the pyramid people may be poor from financial standpoint but not from the intelligence standpoint. By properly nurturing their brain, a huge human resource can be created to help advance the whole world in a coherent way.

Helping "Design for the bottom 90%":

Today, most of the world's products are designed for the rich top 10% to 15% people who can easily afford a high price. But majority of the people (85% to 90%) cannot afford the products designed for the rich. Who can really design some products that will help the bottom of the people? It is most possibly the people from the bottom of the pyramid as they know their problems more than anybody else. Besides, they can also create new industry, new market etc as their Internet usage type would be different and hence they will come up with new ideas of using the Internet to their key benefits.

Ensuring Social Inclusion:

The Digital Divide has caused many people to be isolated from society. Such people feel frustrated as they cannot contribute much, their dignity is affected and their opportunities have become limited. Bridging the Digital Divide will help such population to enjoy most of the benefits that all the people on the other side of the Digital Divide have been enjoying.

For example, many Governments are moving into Digital fast. Thus all the key information and processes including public records (land related forms, birth certificates and the like), bill payment, e-Procurement, job services and the like are converted into electronic form. Such information is not available to people who do not have access to the Internet.

Help minimize the Rich-Poor Gap:

By generating a huge human resource worldwide, many more people would be able to use their knowledge and capabilities to increase earnings and to get out of poverty or become richer. Thus, bridging the Digital Divide will minimize the rich-poor gap.

Clearly, bridging the Digital Divide is not only very important but also a responsibility for the people on the "have" side. It is also important for the people on the "have-not" side to cooperate closely with the people on the "have" side to ensure that the Divide is bridged in a true and effective way. Together, we can make it very successful.

Ensuring Accessibility:

This is related to "Social Inclusion" but still deserves a separate description. Many disabled people cannot use a computer or other electronic devices (like a Personal Digital Assistant). Some special software / hardware are needed for such population group to access the information. For example, a blind person uses a Screen Reading software to use a computer. Bridging the Digital Divide in a true sense would need to ensure that people with disabilities can equally access the information.

In general by "Accessibility" one think of the accessibility for the disabled people and also just to provide the necessary equipments (like a computer) and associated software. However, we should think "Accessibility" from a broader perspective. A poor person who cannot access the Internet, basically, has an "Accessibility" issue—similar to the accessibility issue that a person with disability has. Similarly, a person who has a computer but cannot use it because of complexity or other issues, actually has an "Accessibility" issue, although it seems to be a usability issue. This is even true for a person with disability, has a computer & all associated software but still cannot really use it for other reasons.

Thus, when we say "Accessibility", we should include accessibility not just for disabled but also for all other types of people who cannot use the benefits of the Digital age. Similarly, we will include all people who have a device and associated software but still cannot use them because of complexity, usability and the like; this is important as Bridging the Digital Divide should mean to bridge it in a real sense where it is usable and useful.

Chapter 3

Existing Approaches CANNOT Really Bridge the Digital Divide

Existing Approaches to Bridge the Digital Divide

There are numerous efforts going on worldwide to help bridge the Digital Divide and use ICT for the development. Such approaches mainly use the following:

Device, Connectivity and Content. There are also efforts to help people learn and use computer and Internet.

1. Device

A device is an equipment that users can use to access and interact with the Internet. Providing a device, especially, in an affordable way is the first step in help bridging the Digital Divide. Devices can be classified into 4 broad groups, namely,

1. a regular computer (various organizations, companies, . . . provide such computers to schools, colleges, universities, tele-centers and the like).
2. A low cost simple computers (or similar devices) with very limited but specific capabilities (example—simputer).
3. Personal devices (like PDAs and cell phones).
4. TV with set-top box.

2. Connectivity

Connectivity means connecting a device to the Internet. There are various ways an Internet enabled device can be connected to the Internet—e.g. dial-up, broadband (wire-line broadband using a phone line or cable, wireless broadband), T-1 or E-1line.

3. Content

Content in local languages are keys as people, in general, are much more comfortable to enjoy and use content in local languages.

In addition, trainings on how to use a computer and how to use the Internet are needed so that one can learn how to use the Internet successfully. As mentioned above, there are also various efforts going on worldwide by many organizations to help people learn and use computer and Internet.

Key Issues with the Existing Approaches:

There are some key issues with existing approaches that include above mentioned three key aspects and a few more as described below:

A. Device

Computers (includes regular computers as well as low cost computers):

Computers have revolutionized the world during last decades. These are undoubtedly great devices but making them available to many people in this world has been a big issue. There are various reasons for this. The key reasons are:

Cost—not many people can afford to buy a computer. Even though the prices are coming down steadily, still it would be beyond reach for many people, especially in the developing and 3rd world countries.

It is important to note that many organizations and corporations are providing free computers to various organizations (including NGOs, schools, tele-centers and other institutions). They use both direct as well as other distribution channels to deliver such computers. These are all very good initiatives. Tele-center itself is helping many more people to enjoy the benefits of computers and Internet. Yet, these approaches will not be able to include many people at the bottom of the pyramid. In other words, computers still will be beyond reach for many people for a long time. A good comparison is with electricity which was invented over 100 years ago. But still 28% people in today's world do not have electricity.

Difficulty in Learning—although for some people it is not very difficult to learn how to use a computer, for many people in this world learning how to use a computer is a key issue. This is specifically true for people who have completed school education but did not use a computer (e.g. Learning Operating System, various applications and Internet (more on this follows later in this Section) is not easy to learn for such people).

This is less of a problem for new generation who get exposed to computers at schools from their early childhood. And, this is a major issue for many people who do not know how to read or write (see "Literacy Need" below).

For some people who already learned how to use a computer, it is often difficult to keep on learning new things that come on a regular basis—like dealing with pop-ups, new virus software, new spyware or adware software, new application software, various alerts, dealing with networking issues and the like.

Difficulty in using—many people, especially elderly, blind and other disabled people, who may have learned how to use a computer, find it difficult to use the display screen and keyboard as they grow older.

In addition, we have difficulty in using a browser. Too many links on a page, frames, tables, forms, multimedia, flash, on-click-mouseover, repeating the same links on the page arrived after clicking a link, moving banner s and the like, make the use of a browser difficult for many users. On top this, we have difficulty in selecting specific content from a search results, figuring out what words and their combination can give more desired search results on the first page of search results.

Besides, when mobile (like while driving or walking), one cannot use a computer.

Low cost simple computers—Good for some people but limited capability may cause problems. Low cost definitely helps but the other problems mentioned above still exist, some times with new problems like slower speed, less accessibility, limited features—e.g. a tablet PC does not have a keyboard and so user would need to use many "select" screens and soft keys which is not easy for many people to navigate, fill forms or do transactions.

Maintenance is difficult and expensive—For many people when a computer gets infected with virus or spyware, it is difficult and expensive to fix. In many cases, a user either would like to talk to some customer support person over the phone while following instructions to help recover his / her computer, or just call some support person to come at his/her premise. The latter is more expensive but much easier for the users as users usually would not like to deal with these issues. The former is much more difficult for many people.

Personal Devices:

Personal devices (like cell phones, PDAs) also have revolutionized the world and have added many more people, especially from the bottom of the pyramid, to enjoy the benefits of the information age. Like computers, such devices also have various key issues.

The first such issue is the difficult User Interface. Small screen and small keypad make the usage difficult for many people, especially, as people get older. Limited content is another key issue. There are over 3 billion websites. Re-writing them with another language (for example, in WML or CHTML) so that the content can be viewed on a cell phone screen would cost over trillion dollars and hence not practical. Besides, if a website is re-written into several small websites of small chunk of content (so that they can be viewed on a cell phone screen), the navigation becomes much more difficult. For example, if a regular website has 100 pages and these pages are broken into, say 1000 small pages, then to navigate to 999th page would take a long tree of selection process; thus making it almost impossible to use. PDAs can access any website as is (i.e. no re-writing of a website into small websites is needed) but the whole page does not fit on the screen (or if it fits, it makes it very difficult to view the content in a meaningful way). Thus, users would need to scroll to determine what content to read, making the navigation and finding the desired content difficult.

Besides, for many people, learning all key features of a high end mobile phone or a PDA and associated applications is not simple.

Finally, personal devices (like computers) cannot be used while moving, driving etc. as our eyes and hands are busy in such situations.

Cost is also a major issue for many people.

Another key issue (especially with people from the base of the pyramid) is the use of touch screen. When nothing is displayed, such users do not know what to press to get the initial screen so that they can get started. This becomes more difficult in the dark. A hard button or keypad is more user friendly to such users.

Television with a Set-top Box:

Accessing the Internet via a TV and set-top box has not been very successful yet. However, it has a great promise. With TVs becoming more interactive devices, people getting more and more familiar with the Internet and more attractive content becoming available through digital TV and IPTV, Internet access via TV shows great potential. The cost issue and fear of learning how to use a computer will be significantly minimized for many people.

However, most of the other key issues mentioned above will still apply—like digital TV will still be beyond reach by many people at the base of the pyramid, learning how to use complex features will still be there via a complex remote control.

B. Connection:

Getting Internet connection is another key issue, specially, with broadband—many places do not have broadband connection or if they have, it may be very slow. It would take a very long time before developing and third world countries will have broadband, especially, in rural areas. Modem based access may be slow or may not work well. Wireless broadband, Wi-Max might be good alternatives but still will have speed, availability and cost issues.

C. Learning the Internet:

This true for all devices—computer, PDA, cell phone and TV users. It is not easy for many people, especially who are new to learn what the Internet is, how to learn it, how to use it and how to relate it to their day to day activities. Busy multimedia websites with all types of content, flashes, pop-ups, long navigation tree and the like make it difficult to find desired content, navigate to appropriate content on a linked page and hence difficult to make a good use of it. Many websites organize content where the desired content may be over 3 levels down. For such new users navigating down to over one level is a big issue. The repetitive navigation links common in many web pages is confusing to many new Internet users. Form filling (especially complex sequential forms used in complex applications) is difficult for many users—e.g. when a form is filled, another form pops up along with other content and forms on the new page. In such a scenario, a user may not be sure which form to select. In many cases, the labels of the form are not clear to users who do not have much knowledge about the Internet or about the specific application. With the advances in dynamic content concepts and associated programming languages (DHTML, Ajax, and the like), suddenly new windows or screens pop up asking questions which many users do not know what to do about. Many also do not know how to kill such windows. Downloading some desired files also present complexity—e.g. when a link is clicked to download a desired file / program, bunch of other download options (specially driven by advertisement) are presented, making it complex for many users. Such problems will not go away as websites designed for advanced users will remain difficult to be properly used by simple users.

D. Literacy Need:

To use a computer, PDA, cell phone or a TV for Internet access, one needs to know how to read and write. However, many people at the bottom of the pyramid do not know how to read or write. This is a huge problem as literacy rate for base of the pyramid people, in general, is very low. Many do not go to school. Even though various efforts are going on by various organizations including Governments, NGOs, and UNESCO to improve the literacy rate worldwide, it will take long time before most people at the bottom of the pyramid will learn how to read and write.

E. Content

Although content is growing everyday, most of the Internet content is still in English (about 70%). So, people in non-English speaking countries are deprived from major part of the Internet. Content in Chinese are growing fast but that will not be useful by non-Chinese speaking people. This has caused a huge gap or divide called Language Divide. Some websites provide content in multiple languages and some websites allow users to get translation engine to translate content in another language. These are definitely good efforts. But many users do not know how to get and use a translation engine to translate the content. More importantly, very few content is available that meet the needs of the base of the pyramid people. Such desired missing content will not be developed automatically. It has to come from the people at the base of the pyramid in a way that will help improve their economic and social conditions, which in most cases would also need a good sustainable business model.

Why Existing Approaches CANNOT Really Bridge the Digital Divide

As clear from the analysis above, existing approaches can bridge the Digital Divide only to a limited extent. Many people, especially, from the bottom of the pyramid will not be able to use existing approaches to enjoy the benefits of the Internet. Out of over 6.8 Billion people in the world, today about little bit over a billion people can access the Internet using computers and other devices. Continuing in the same way will increase users at a relatively slow rate. So, may be in 10 years another billion will get some sort of Internet Access. But majority will still be left out as they either would not have a computer, or would not be able to learn how to use it, or would not have the Internet access or would not be literate enough etc.

Since mobile devices are ubiquitous and still growing fast, it makes more sense to use mobile phones to provide the internet to lot more people. At the time of this writing, there are over 5 billion phones (over 4 billion mobile phones and over a billion wire-line phones) worldwide. If we can provide the Internet through such devices, then we can easily reach significantly much more people. However, existing approaches will not be able to provide Internet to all mobile phones in a meaningful way. There are quite a few reasons for that.

First, is the affordability. As of today about 15% of the mobile phone has Internet capability but in a limited way as described above—user interface is difficult, content is limited, navigation is difficult etc. It is unlikely that most cell phone will have Internet capability in the near future. And even if most cell phone will have limited Internet capability in the near future, many people would not be able to afford it.

Secondly, many people would not be able to use it because of literacy issue. As already mentioned, it will take long time before most people in this world will become literate.

Thirdly, because of the difficult user interface and navigation difficulty, yet many other users would not be able to use it.

Fourthly, content will remain limited as it is economically infeasible to re-write the whole World Wide Web content in another language. Creating new content on the Wireless web is only feasible to a limited extent because of cost of development and difficulty in navigation. Mobile phone websites with too many pages will cause a long navigation tree, making it unusable or difficult to use. These are the key reasons for which mobile applications are successfully addressing only specific (but good) problems but not addressing mobile general content rich websites like the websites on the World Wide Web.

Thus, no matter how we cut it, existing approaches DO NOT and CANNOT solve the key problems, namely,

1. providing computer to everyone is not feasible
2. computers are not affordable by many people
3. computers are difficult to learn
4. computers are difficult to use
5. power supply can be a big issue in many parts of the world
6. difficult to navigate (especially in a mobile phone)
7. computers or other visual display not usable when mobile (eyes busy and hand busy)
8. one would need to know how to read and write
9. re-writing all websites to fit on a small screen in a cell phone is not practical as there are over 3 billion websites and it would cost over trillion dollars to re-write.
   Even if all websites could be re-written, the navigation would be impossible as the navigation tree to cover all content on a website will be too long

In fact, it is clear that the Digital Divide is actually widening considering all possible aspects—yes, for some aspects the Divide is getting minimized, e.g. gaps between some developing countries and rich countries; but for most aspects, the Divide is growing, especially between the Bottom of the Pyramid people and the rich people.

Hence, some different approaches should be used that can solve all the key problems mentioned, and thus really help bridge the Digital Divide. Next few chapters provide some good solutions to these problems and provide some practical solutions to significantly narrow the Digital Divide gap.

Determining What is Economical

Since, existing approaches (although very important and should be continued) alone cannot bridge the Digital Divide, and we would need to use other approaches (especially Voice Internet) to effectively bridge the Digital Divide, it is very important to look into the economics of these approaches. Existing approaches, especially using broadband, wi-max, wi-fi hotspots can be expensive to many developing and underdeveloped countries if they would like to cover the whole region, say with broadband. The same is true with mobile networks as well—mobile networks, especially at remote locations are expensive / not cost effective for many developing countries since only few can afford high end phones and many cannot afford even low cost mobile phones in such countries. Since covering a whole region with broadband (or mobile network) will still leave many people on the other side of the Digital Divide unable to access the information, a much lower cost alternatives (e.g. Voice Internet as explained in more details in Part II) should be explored. It costs far less for Voice Internet as existing telecom infrastructure will be used to make a regular phone call (i.e. voice and not data). Good Internet connection would be needed ONLY at the central location(s) where servers will be hosted. No broadband or Internet connection will be needed at user's location as user will make a regular phone call using a landline or mobile phone. Users would not need to buy a special phone or data package. More importantly, users would get the whole Internet content as no re-writing of websites would be needed. Besides, no reading-writing literacy would be needed as user's will be talking and listening to the Internet.

Since resource, in general, is always limited, a Government should carefully consider in utilizing its resources the best way possible. Strategies, models and approaches that have been prescribed for a developed country may not be appropriate for an underdeveloped or developing country. For example, covering a country completely with broadband may work well for a developed country where Digital Divide is relatively small, resources is available, affordability is not a major issue and many users are literate. For an underdeveloped country, on the other hand, this would not make sense as literacy rate is very low (in general), poverty is high, affordability is a big issue, and Digital Divide is huge. So, by providing computers and broadband may help only relatively rich people in the country leaving most people un-served. Whereas, using a low cost alternative which needs much less investment, is easy to learn, easy to use, very affordable and does not need literacy, would make perfect sense. With such initial, low investment, many people at the Base of the Pyramid would be able to learn the benefits of using information, apply it to their day to day life with special focus on education, innovation and entrepreneurship as related to their life; and thus help improve their economic, social and cultural situation. This will also enable them to spend more to eventually buy a computer, getting broadband Internet access and thus help achieve further growth.

Of course, many of them may just decide to continue use the low cost alternative (like Voice Internet) as they may not be comfortable in learning how to read and write and complete formal education.

Thus, for developing and underdeveloped countries, a low cost alternative (e.g. Voice Internet) can be much more affordable, logical and appropriate along with limited broadband in key locations. This will help a country's valuable resources to be utilized more economically and effectively.

PART TWO

The Way to Truly Bridging the Digital Divide

Chapter 4

Approaches to really Bridge the
Digital Divide—Technology and Solution

The key limitations of existing approaches can be summarized to (as described in detail in Chapter 3)

1. not affordable by many people
2. not available in many areas (lack of connectivity)
3. difficult to learn
4. difficult to use
5. difficult to find desired content
6. difficult to navigate
7. not usable when mobile (eyes busy and hand busy situation)
8. one would need to know how to read and write
9. lack of content for many people, especially at the base of the pyramid

All these issues can be addressed by using a simple telephone and user's voice. Instead of using a small screen display to view the content, a user can listen to the content. Instead of using a key board or keypad, a user can just talk. Instead of learning difficult user interface, difficult navigation process to get to the appropriate content, a user get the desired content in an automated way. Thus, a user can surf any website, search any topic, send/receive/compose/delete email, conduct e-ecommerce, listen to streaming audio (music or Internet radios) and much more just by talking and listening. For example, to surf Yahoo website, a user would do the following:

A. Say "surf the net"
B. Select Yahoo website by saying "Yahoo"
C. Listen to the yahoo web content

This process of providing content from visual internet into meaningful audio content by using any phone and user's voice is called **Voice Internet**. It is basically talking and listening to the Internet in a very effective way by using the most ubiquitous device, a simple phone and the best user interface, one's own voice. Voice Internet allows a user to listen to any internet website content in a manner that the content **is short, precise, easily navigable, meaningful and pleasant to listen to,** using any phone and user's voice. There is no need to re-write the website content. Voice Internet, basically overcomes all the limitations of existing approaches i.e.

a. a computer is not needed
b. a high end phone or PDA is not needed
c. a phone (especially) simple phone is much easier to learn and use
d. no re-writing of website (there are over 3 Billion websites and re-writing them would be cost prohibitive and impractical)
e. can be used in an eyes busy hands busy situation
f. can be used by anyone without knowing how to read and write
g. can be used while mobile (in an eyes busy, hands busy situation)

Thus, Voice Internet "truly bridges the Digital Divide" in a cost effective way.

The idea of listening to the Internet may at first sounds a bit like watching the radio. How does a visual medium rich in icons, text, and images translate itself into an audible format that is meaningful and pleasing to the ear? The answer lies in an innovative integration of three distinct technologies that **render** visual content into short, precise, easily navigable, and meaningful text that can be converted to audio.

The three technologies employed to accomplish this feat are:

1. Speech recognition
2. Text-to-speech translation, and
3. Web content rendering

What is rendering?

Merriam-Webster Unabridged defines rendering as "a work forming a presentation, expression, or interpretation (as of an idea, theme, or part)". Information technology uses this term to refer to how information is presented according to the medium, for example, graphically displayed on a screen, audibly read using a recording device, or printed on a piece of paper.

In the context of voice/audio Internet, Web content rendering entails the translation of information originally intended for visual presentation into a format more suitable to audio. Conceptually this is quite a straightforward process but tactically, it poses some daunting challenges in executing this translation. What are those challenges and why are they so difficult to overcome? These questions are explored in the next section.

The rendering problem

Computers possess certain superhuman attributes, which far outstrip that of mortal man—most notable are their computational capabilities. The common business spreadsheet is a testament to this fact. Other seemingly more mundane tasks, however, present quite a conundrum for even the most sophisticated of processors. Designing a high-speed special purpose computer capable of defeating a grandmaster at chess took the computing industry over 50 years to perfect. Employing strategic thinking is not a computer's forte. That is because in all the logic embodied in their digitized ones and zeroes, there is no inherent cognitive thought. This one powerful achievement of the brain along with our ability to feel and express emotion separates the human mind from its computerized equivalent—the centralized processing unit (CPU).

It is doubtful (and academically arguable) whether or not computers may one day be capable of expressing emotion but computer scientists have been struggling with the issue of developing cognitive thought and have made surprising progress over the years. The branch of computing involved in this pursuit is known as Artificial Intelligence. It is a field rife with "buzz words" such as, fuzzy logic, neural networks, adaptive control, and stochastic reasoning.

The relevance of cognitive thought to text rendering may not be immediately obvious but it is one of the major challenges faced when attempting to present information designed for one medium and rendering it to another. This is because there are no hard and fast objective rules to follow. Computers are very good at following instructions when they can be reduced to very objective decision points. They are not so good when value judgments are involved. A human being can readily distinguish a cat from a dog, or a relevant news link on a Web page from a link for an advertisement. For a computer this simple exercise is significantly more challenging than applying the Taylor expansion formula to a set of polynomials—something a computer can do quite handily.

Navigating a Web page is very similar in process to reading a newspaper. We immediately note the lead story, scan headlines, and then select a story of interest to us. Once we begin reading a news item we inevitably must turn to an inside page and specific column to finish the story. This is the Internet equivalent of linking to another page with a mouse click. Having performed that link our brain processes the visual clues on the next Web page to begin reading where the previous page left off—easy for us but not so easy for a computer.

Solving the problem

To solve the rendering problem, some intelligent techniques must be applied. The relevant data must be selected, navigated to its conclusion, and reassembled for presentation by a different medium. All of this must be done for all web pages, dynamically, in real-time and in an automated fashion. **Voice Internet** uses an Intelligent Agent (IA) that uses various intelligent techniques including "artificial intelligence" to solve this rendering problem.

Using Visual Clues

Understanding the process that our brains go through in making qualitative choices is key to developing an artificially intelligent solution. In the example of Web page navigation we know that our brains do not attempt to read and interpret an entire page of data rather they take their cues from the visual clues implemented by the Web designer. These clues include such things as placement of text, use of color, size of font, density of content and meaning of a word(s). From these clues a list of potential areas of interest can be developed and presented as a list of candidates.

Upon selecting an item of interest it is common to have to navigate to another Web page to read all the data of interest (just like in the newspaper example). To do so we click on a Web link. When following a page link the problem of continuity of thought is encountered because almost assuredly the newly linked page contains data in addition to the thread of information we are attempting to follow. In order to maintain continuity with the item from the previous page a contextual correlation must be made. Once again, this cognitive process poses a formidable challenge for the computer and requires application of Intelligent Agent (or artificial intelligence) principles to solve.

Simplifying for speech

The first step involves dynamically removing all the programming constructs and coding tags that comprise the instruction to a Web browser on how to visually render the data. HTML, CHTML, XML, and other languages are typically used for this purpose. Because the data is now being translated or rendered to a different medium, these tags no longer serve any purpose.

It is doubtful that every single data item on a page will be read. Just like reading a newspaper, we read only items of interest and generally skip advertisements completely. Thus, we need to automatically render important information on a page and then when a topic is selected, only the relevant information from the linked page corresponding to the selected topic needs to be presented. Rendering is achieved by using Page Highlights (using a method to find and speak the key content on a page), finding right as well as only relevant content on a linked page, assembling appropriate content from a linked page, and providing easy navigation.

Finding and Assembling Relevant Information

To find relevant information, the Intelligent Agent (IA) uses various deterministic and non-deterministic algorithms that use contextual and non-contextual matches, semantic analysis, and learning. This is again very similar to how we do use our eyes and brain to find the relevant content. To ensure real-time performance, algorithms are simplified as needed yet producing very satisfactory results. Once relevant content are determined, they are assembled in appropriate order that makes sense when listen to in audio or viewed on a small screen.

How Well Does the Rendering Work?

To answer how well the 'rendering' and Voice Internet can provide meaningful content from today's Internet, we need to answer the following questions:

(1) can the content really be provided from any web site on the Internet?

(2) can the existing Internet content be rendered in a manner that the rendered content can be obtained in real time, is short, precise, easy to navigate, meaningful in audio and pleasant to listen?

The answers to both questions are "yes". Depending on the site, the "yes" can be a very strong "yes" or a strong "yes" a weak "yes". A content rich page with a small number of links makes rendering and navigation easy since there are only a few choices, and one can quickly select a particular topic or section. If the site is rich in content, links and images/graphics, the problem is more difficult but good solution still exists by carefully selecting a built-in feature called "Page Highlights" as described before. The most difficult case is when a page is very rich in images/graphics and links. In such cases, the main information is located several levels down from the home page and so navigation becomes more difficult as one has to go through multiple levels. Using multi-level Page Highlights and customized Highlights, the content can still be rendered well. But in this case, it is not as easy to navigate as the other two cases. Usually most of the Internet content falls under the first and second categories.

netECHO: an Example of Voice Internet [Courtesy InternetSpeech, Inc]

Here's how InternetSpeech has given a voice to the Internet. Voice Internet technology, netECHO®, uses an Intelligent Agent (IA) [Fig. 4.1] as described above that transforms an ordinary telephone into a high-tech tool for accessing the Internet. A user calls the service, is greeted by the IA. The IA then provides a menu of items to choose content from the Internet. The user can surf any website, search for sites or information using search word(s), send and receive email, and conduct e-commerce. In addition, common voice portal features, such as news, weather, horoscopes and directions can be quickly accessed from a menu of items. Users can give simple commands, such as "go to Yahoo" or "read my email" to get to the net-based information they want, when they want it, whether they're out on an appointment, stuck in traffic, sitting in an airport, or cooking dinner. Users can quickly locate information, such a late-breaking news, traffic reports, directions, or anything else they're interested in on the World Wide Web.

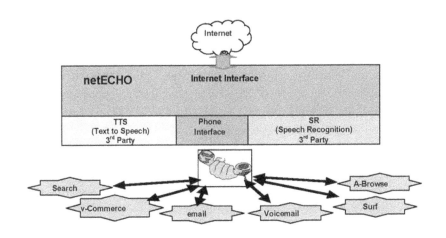

Fig. 4.1 The Intelligent Agent (IA) and Key Features of net ECHO®

This automated way of accessing any content from the Internet using an Intelligent Agent is the key to creating a voice Internet that doesn't require re-writing of the websites. The IA dynamically translates the accessed web pages into speech. There is no limit to the sites you can access, since all common markups languages (HTML, WML, XML, VoiceXML, etc) are supported. The IA evaluates the site and determines which information is most useful and meaningful ("rendering"), then presents the content in easy-to-follow chunks using the "Page Highlights" feature. The system takes the caller to the selected content on a linked page with easy navigation by simply saying which link he/she wants after being given a short list of choices.

A similar software Intelligent Agent is also used for business-to-business and government applications that let a company's customers hear and interact with their website (or web based applications) from any phone, without a computer. The software allows customers to retrieve product and pricing information, check an order or account status, purchase products, or obtain product support, etc., using their own voice.

The work that has been accomplished to date makes the majority of sites very useful, and with customization, allows for further interaction with the site for e-commerce and other complex form filling applications.

More Details on the Key Features of Voice Internet, netECHO®

Voice Internet has all the key features of the Visual Internet including surfing, searching, doing email, conducting e-commerce and listening to streaming audio. Voice Internet also supports Voice Portal features like stock quote, weather, news, horoscope using the content directly from the Internet, instead of using different sources of content as usually used in the Voice Portal approach.

As mentioned above, good 'rendering' is the key to effectively provide content from the Internet over any phone. Today's Internet was designed with the idea that primary access to it would be through a visual means. Accordingly, all the information is laid out in a manner that attracts our eyes but not ears. To make it meaningful and useful while listening, a very good "rendering" *process is required as mentioned above. The **"rendering"** process converts the content from the Internet into **short, precise, easily navigable and meaningful content in real time**. It automatically generates **highlights** of the page and presents them in a small amount of information at a time that one can easily follow. Once a highlight is selected, the relevant content from the linked page (or current page) are automatically found and rendered in a small amount of information as mentioned above. Users can easily navigate within and between pages using simple voice commands or keypad entry.*

Voice Internet also supports two other modes:

(a) *Link Mode*—When Link Mode is enabled, netECHO alerts, by saying "LINK", after each time it reads a word (or words) that have a hyperlink associated with it. There is a brief pause, during which you can choose to navigate "down" the link, by saying "That One" or "yes" or pressing "1". If you say nothing, netECHO continues reading-out the text.

This mode is similar to Screen Reader mode where all the content is read from top to the bottom of the page.

(b) *Default Mode* (non Highlight and non-Link Mode)—in this mode all the content on a page are read without making announcement of any link and without allowing to go to any link. This mode is mainly used for the Voice Portal features like used for email, stock quote, horoscope etc.

Surfing and Browsing the Web

Voice Internet (e.g. netECHO˚ from InternetSpeech) allows you to surf and browse any website in audio. After you provide the website address, netECHO downloads the website content and automatically renders the content into meaningful small amount using the above mentioned "rendering" concept. You can easily navigate from page to page or within a page. You can bookmark and save your favorite websites by spelling them once. A website address can be selected in 4 ways:

a) Popular Website

b) Bookmarked Website
c) Spelling by Voice
d) Spelling by Keypad Entry

If (c) or (d) is used, you will have the option to save the spelled website into a Bookmark.

Web Search

You can search any word(s) using any search engine. Once you spell the desired search word(s), netECHO provides an option to save the word(s) and then presents the search results using the rendering method mentioned above. It also supports on-page search and on-site search.

Email

You can access your email accounts, using your own voice. netECHO's intelligent agent "reads-out" the text of your email, providing instant access to critical information, anywhere, anytime. You can also compose, delete, reply, forward, and send copies of your emails to others. In replying or composing an email, you can either use voice or text. For voice reply, you just naturally say your reply. It goes as a voice attachment. For text reply, you can spell your response using the telephone keypad or by voice. Both upper case and lower case letters are supported.

Popular Services / Voice Portal Features

netECHO also provides direct access to important services like news, stock quotes, horoscopes, directory assistance (including Yellow Page and White Page), religion, and weather.

Steaming Audio

Many websites have streaming audio. netECHO supports all major streaming audio formats. Thus, you can listen to on-line music and Internet radios.

Shopping

On-line shopping is becoming more and more popular. Voice Internet supports on-line shopping and other type of on-line transactions.

Social Networks

Voice Internet net ECHO has simple special interface for Social websites like Twitter and Facebook.

e-Services & Other Key Features

Custom version of net ECHO supports various e-Services including e-Gov., e-Learning, e-Health and e-Agriculture. Custom Voice Internet (more detailed description is provided in the **Custom Voice Internet** *Section below*) also supports almost all features on the Internet with simpler user interface. This works like whole Internet as an IVR (Interactive Voice Response) system.

In addition, netECHO includes key features like **Page Highlights, Traversing Links, Previous Page, Next Paragraph, and Skip Paragraph** to ensure easy and seamless navigation. It supports uppercase letters to allow users to compose more professional text emails.

How Users Are Using Voice Internet?

Voice Internet, netECHO current users are using most of the features mentioned above. The top three mostly used features are:

1. email (35-40% of the time)
2. surfing (20%, up to 50% when streaming audio is used)
3. searching (15%, up to 30% when streaming audio is used)

About $1/3^{rd}$ of the current users pay additional amount to listen to the streaming audio.

Users call multiple times a day. The duration of each phone call depends on the type of users. Table 4.1 shows average duration per call for various types of users. The number of times users call in a day varies from 4-6 on the average.

Every user has a list of websites in the Bookmark. Users update the bookmark list on a regular basis. This can be done by spelling the website using voice or telephone keypad.

Similarly, every user has a list of email addresses in the email address book. Email addresses can be entered and updated by spelling by voice or telephone keypad. A special feature called 'mynetECHO" allows a user to pre-configure favorite features like email, weather, and horoscope. With mynetECHO, users get all the pre-selected features just by saying mynetECHO without selecting each features separately.

Type of Users	Average Minutes Used Per Phone Call
Visually Impaired / Blind people	30
Elderly People	16
Digital Divide People	12
Highly Mobile People	4

Table 4.1: Average duration per call for various types of users.

To ensure that users can get to the desired content faster and easier, the netECHO menu is selected in a manner so that number of levels to reach any content is small, usually ranging from 0-3. For example, (a) information on how to use the service can be obtained just by saying E-Z Guide with zero level of traversing and (b) a word can be searched with two levels of traversing—first level to reach the search results as Page Highlights and the second level (may third level depending on the type of search results found) to listen to the desired content. Table 4.2 below shows how a user uses the Surfing feature.

Search feature is used for searching various topics. The most common topics are cooking, diseases, songs, and name of important articles.

The Dictionary, Directory Assistance, On-Line Book Reading, Bible, horoscope and Weather are the most important voice portal features are used everyday many times.

Surf the Net (with Highlight Mode Enabled)

- *User says: 'Surf the Net' at the Main Menu*
- netECHO reads the Surf the Net sub-menu
- *User says: 'Popular Website'*
- netECHO says: Please say your popular Website
- *User says: 'Yahoo'*
- netECHO confirms yahoo.com and provides the Highlights of the Page
- User selects a Highlight by saying "second one", for example.
- netECHO goes to the desired page and reads the relevant content; it says **'link'** when it finds a link
- *User chooses link by saying 'that one'*
- netECHO downloads the selected Linked page and starts reading it

User listens **and selects more links or after a while, presses "**" to go back to the Main Menu or presses "#7" to go back to the previous page.**

Table 4.2: How the Surfing works in Voice Internet, netECHO

Streaming Audio is another very heavily used feature. Users use this feature to listen to on-line music and Internet Radio stations. Users usually stay over 30 minutes per call when this feature is used.

A new user unfamiliar with the Internet usually starts with email & streaming audio, and then learns how to do surfing and searching. Such a user usually learns most of the basic stuff in 3-7 days. A user familiar with the Internet usually learns how to use the Voice Internet in 1-2 days. Thus, Customer Support is easier and does not take much time. Key questions a Customer Support usually answers are:

a) what is the Internet and what is a website?
b) what is the difference between surfing and searching
c) how to enter an email address in the email addressbook

d) how to bookmark a website

e) how to find free music or Internet radio stations using the search feature

Custom Voice Internet

General Voice Internet described above supports all key features of the Internet including surfing, searching, email and some e-commerce. General Voice Internet also supports basic form filling to logon or sign-up on a website by using the command "Form Filling".

For complex applications like general e-commerce and transactions, complex form filling is used. However, for sequential complex form filling (e.g. in an e-commerce application), there may be quite a few forms to be filled. Filling such forms in a general way (by using "Form Filling" command in net ECHO) is not natural to many users, especially, at the base of the pyramid. Besides, the dialogues to complete the process are also not natural for many users. To avoid this type of problem and make the process very natural, easy to use and enjoyable, Custom Voice Internet option is used. In such scheme, the dialogues are made natural, all forms are automatically presented in the appropriate sequence and dialogue is tuned for the application. Thus, for a banking application, the dialogues would be specific to banking as shown below. No option would be given for surfing, searching, email etc (unless specifically requested by the Bank). Sample dialogue for a banking applications is shown in Table 4.3.

Custom Voice Internet uses the same "rendering engine" and Intelligent Agent used in the general Voice Internet. Only the dialogue and some features of the "rendering" are customized. It usually takes a few days to a few weeks to develop a Custom Voice Internet, depending on the complexity of the applications. For simple applications, changes in the dialogue can be done by the developer (customer). For complex applications, it is usually better if InternetSpeech does the customization in consultation with the customer. Custom Voice Internet service, like, general Voice Internet service can be hosted by the customer or by any 3rd party hosting company.

- net ECHO says, *"Welcome to Banking Application Powered by InternetSpeech. Would you like to check balance, transfer money or apply for a loan?"*
- User says: "transfer money"
- n*et ECHO says: "from which account to which account?"*
- *u*ser says, "from savings to check-in"
- net ECHO says, "please say the amount"
- *User says: "**one hundred dollars"***
- netECHO says: "your requested transfer is completed. Would you like to do another transaction?"
- User says: "no"
- net ECHO says: "thank you for using our Voice Internet Banking service"

Table 4.3 Sample Dialogue for a Banking Application using Voice Internet, netECHO

There can be many Custom Voice Internet services—for example, CRM, Travel Reservation, Air Line Booking, Package tracking, bill payment, e-Services (including e-Gov, e-Learning, e-Farming, e-Health) and many more. **However, e-Services** need special attention as they are keys for the base of the pyramid people. Hence, a few e-Services are described in detail in Chapter 6 where Voice Internet deployment issues are emphasized. To clarify the concept of Custom Voice Internet, here we have included Voice Banking, one key popular custom application of Voice Internet, netECHO®.

Voice Banking Application—an imperative

Faced with steadily rising operating costs and competition in providing the best customer services, service industries like Banking and Insurance need new techniques for improving efficiency and finding successful channels to deliver consistent, outstanding customer service. Customer self-service through the Web provides a partial solution, but this approach does not accommodate the many customers for whom network access is inconvenient or impractical.

IVR products have been available for many years to automate call processing, but before speech-driven systems, they were exclusively based on Dual Tone Multi-Frequency (DTMF), otherwise known as touch-tones. Applications built on these platforms provided a good return on investment (ROI), but often frustrated callers with lengthy menus and arcane command sequences. Another issue with DTMF driven IVRs is getting "lost in the maze." If the callers' option does not appear at one level, or they press the wrong key, the caller is likely to be stranded in another department. By the time the caller is finally transferred to the correct department, they have had an unpleasant experience, or have hung up.

The challenge is therefore, to develop a pleasant-to-use, automated, efficient, and cost-effective system that provides information readily, before it transfers the caller to a live operator for help.

Call Centers can now take advantage of recent advancements in speech technology. In most cases, the operating costs of a speech recognition system are about 10 to 20% of a comparable human-powered call center and half to one-third the cost of touch-tone or web systems. Automating contact centers with Voice Internet Technology can deliver a good ROI while raising the level of caller satisfaction. Greater automation rates improve savings further, while greater call-handling capacity reduces hold queue times for better service. Call center agents can function more efficiently and are relieved of tedious, repetitive requests, freeing them to address more intellectually challenging problems.

Other Key Points to Note:

1. *Voice Banking using general Voice Internet Versus Custom Voice Internet The method described above uses Custom Voice Internet for Voice Banking where the net ECHO core "rendering engine" is used with a Custom Front End dialogue that is fine tuned for banking on a specific bank website. However, the Form Filling feature in net ECHO can also be used to do all banking related transactions (like money transfer, account balance and the like). In this case, user would use the general "Form Filling" command as opposed to naturally filling forms using Custom Front End Voice dialogue.*

2. *Security Issue*

    Obviously, password and user id are not secured in any voice system. To ensure that we have a secured banking application in net ECHO with two options:

    (a) *Using Caller ID (i.e. ANI—Automatic Number Identification) so that a user would need to call from some specific pre-registered phone number).*
    (b) *Additional security steps / questions if a user is allowed to use any phone number.*

3. *Regulatory Issue*

    Some countries might have some regulatory issues which can easily be addressed by discussion / negotiation. There might be need for some related technical implementation which netECHO can easily accommodate.

Chapter 5

What is the Language Divide
and How to Bridge It

The Digital Divide issue has been talked about in depth in many literatures. However, there is another Divide, called the Language Divide, of similar magnitude which has not been really discussed or talked about. Over 70% of the Internet content today is written in English. So, people in countries like China, India, Japan, Russia are left out from the major part of the internet as they do not prefer to use English or many of them do not even know English. This divide is called the Language Divide. It has some overlap with multi-lingual support that has been talked about in some literatures.

Language Divide has other implications—in a few years Chinese content on the Internet will grow to a significant level. People not speaking Chinese will not be able to access the Chinese part of the WWW. This can be extended to other languages as well. In general, in this global world, people not only need to access websites in all languages (the main focus of the multi-lingual approach) but also need to understand the content of the websites in all other languages. Thus, bridging the Language Divide is equally important as bridging the Digital Divide. In other words, bridging the Digital Divide will not be complete if the "Language Divide" is not bridged as well.

To bridge the Language Divide, we would need automated translation to translate web content from one language into other languages, which is called **Machine Translation (MT)**. Automated translation, unfortunately, has not reached a point where the translation is highly accurate. This is more true when a book is translated from one language to another using a translation software. The error level, in most cases, is not acceptable. **This is mainly because of the fact that the machine translation (MT) is a very complex problem and the solution is not just there yet.**

However, in translating web pages, the problem is much less complex as a website usually has simple sentences and paragraphs. So, current MT can provide reasonably good results in many cases. But it is important to note that much more work is needed in machine translation to really bridge the Language Divide. **So, when we say bridging Language Divide, we mean bridging it using the state of the art technologies that exist today with limited translation capability that we can rely upon. But it is still better than not translating at all.**

It is also important to note that even when a very reliable MT becomes available for any topic in the near future, just translating all websites into various languages will not completely bridge the language Divide. This is more true for the base of the pyramid people. People at the bottom of the pyramid are mostly illiterate or semi-literate. The content that exists today on the Internet is more tuned for literate people. This includes:

a) most of the topics
b) the way the content is written and displayed or presented
c) the way content can be searched
d) the way users interact using social networks
e) the way users upload information
f) the way e-Learning courses are offered
g) the way e-Commerce is done
h) and the list goes on.

Besides, as already mentioned, either a computer or a high end phone or similar display device would be needed to access the content.

So, automated translation by MT would help many literate people and possibly some illiterate people but many people at the base of the pyramid will be left out.

Thus, in addition to automated translation by MT, we would need content in local languages in a manner that

a) it address the needs of the local people
b) are in local languages
c) are organized in a manner that is more suitable to access for illiterate people
d) can be found very easily using natural way of asking
e) can be shared in a way that illiterate people are comfortable with
f) presented in a manner that illiterate people can easily achieve literacy and start learning the traditional Internet content

All these imply that we would need Voice Internet and Natural Language based communication (as further described below). Thus, to really bridge the Language Divide, we would need

1. very good MT based translation and
2. local language based content easily accessible and usable
3. a device that is low cost, easy to use and ubiquitous

#2 & #3 will enable base of the pyramid people to gradually successfully use content translated by MT.

Thus, MT's role is still very critical and hence more on MT is covered below.

However, since this is not a book to focus on technical details of MT, I just describe critical issues of MT in a simple non-technical manner, mainly focusing on the complexity of machine translation and its future.

Machine Translation—Complexity

Language translation, in general, is very complex even when done by a human. For example, an amateur translator tends to produce prose that is unnatural, perhaps with mistakes in specialized terminology. An expert human translator does a good job but it needs very good understanding of the language, topic of interest, contexts, writing style among others. Human cognition is key to ensure a good translation from one language into the other. The following points will make it more clear [Jurafsky2010]:

1. Not all the words in one language have equivalent words in another language. In some cases a word in one language is to be expressed by group of words in another.
2. Two given languages may have completely different structures. For example English has SVO (Subject Verb Object) structure while Tamil has SOV (Subject Object Verb) structure.
3. Sometimes there is a lack of one-to-one correspondence of parts of speech between two languages. For example, color terms of Tamil are nouns whereas in English they are adjectives.
4. The way sentences are put together also differ among languages.
5. Words can have more than one meaning and sometimes group of words or whole sentence may have more than one meaning in a language. This problem is called ambiguity.
6. Not all the translation problems can be solved by applying values of grammar.
7. It is too difficult for the software programs to predict meaning.
8. Translation requires not only vocabulary and grammar but also knowledge gathered from past experience.
9. The programmer should understand the rules under which complex human language operates and how the mechanism of this operation can be simulated by automatic means.
10. The simulation of human language behavior by automatic means is almost impossible to achieve (at least with today's conventional known algorithms) as the language is an open and dynamic system in constant change. More importantly the system is not yet completely understood. Computational Linguistics researchers are trying their best to solve this understanding & modeling problem of human language.

In fact, MT complexity is directly related to **NLU** (Natural Language Understanding) complexity which is mainly related to **Semantics**: abstraction, representation, real meaning, and computational complexity [Khan2011]. These i.e. Semantics, NLU and MT are actually three complex open problems that many researchers around the world are trying to solve.

Thus, today, no machine can reliably address the key issues of automated language translation. No machine has the real language understanding, cognition, context, writing style etc. What we have is a some sort of rule based fixed (or partially variable with known rules) structure. We also have some statistical based approaches to translate one language into another using dictionary and grammars. Recently with much larger word training database e.g. Google's over trillion word n-gram dataset [LinkNGRAM], the translation accuracy has improved by a good percentage, especially for some specific contexts. These are all very good systems and used by many people. However, our need is still to have near human like translation capability by machines. Computers, today, cannot really think or understand like a human does. So, the result of MT is usually good for some domain specific and limited vocabulary based applications. For general natural language based topics, MT produces results that can be highly inaccurate.

The translation quality of the machine translation systems can be improved by pre-editing the input. Pre-editing means adjusting the input by marking prefixes, suffixes, clause boundaries, etc. Translation quality can also be improved by controlling the vocabulary. The output of the machine translation should be post-edited to make it perfect. However, when we are talking about MT for website content to be accessed in real-time, pre-editing and post-editing is not practical.

Machine Translation: past, present & future—a short overview

Machine translation efforts dates back to early 1950. Due to the complexity of the problem and high expectation set in the industry, the results were not very encouraging and during its 2nd and 3rd decades many fundings were cut and efforts were at minimum level. However, since late 4th decade (1980), it got revived. With newer technologies like neural networks, fuzzy logic, statistical learning, in the 5th and 6th decades, the translation accuracy got better. But the fundamental problem is not solved yet i.e. the language understanding at human level as mentioned in Chapter 4 (under Section on Robotics and Beyond). In fact, it appears that without using algorithms that our brain uses in doing **language understanding & translation**, it would be very difficult, if not impossible, to make computers do a good job on machine translation. Fortunately, some people have started focusing on this ([Hawkins2004], [Slocum 1985]) and in the near future we expect to see good progress in MT. It is important to note that understanding how our brain does language understanding is very difficult. However, with recent special focus on how our brain works by many researchers around the world using a multi-disciplinary approach should expedite the process significantly. Even with partial understanding of how language understanding is done in our brain, especially in **neo-cortex**, would help us develop a much better MT.

Based on recent research around the world, it is very clear that our brains do not compute using the binary numbers used in today's computers. It also does not solve differential equations in doing arm movements (e.g. when catching a ball) or use signal processing and other statistical algorithms in recognizing an object or in understanding a spoken word(s). What brain uses is some sort of pattern manipulation in solving all sorts of computations. The nature of these patterns is different at different levels and hierarchies.

A good reference in this regard is "On Intelligence" by Jeff Hawkins [Hawkins2004]. The below excerpt Further explains this

"The brain is not a computer, supplying by rote an output for each input it receives. Instead, it is a memory system that stores experiences in a way that reflects the true structure of the world, remembering sequences of events and their nested relationships and making predictions based on those memories. It is the memory-prediction system that forms the basis of intelligence, perception, creativity, and even consciousness. Intelligence is the capacity of the brain to predict the future by analogy to the past".

The MT and natural language understanding part is believed to be mainly done by neo-cortex but with well coordination and contribution from other key 4 lobes in human brain, namely, Frontal, Parietal, Occipital and Temporal. With recent focus on understanding how human brain works by many brain researchers, especially, from multi-disciplinary angle involving cognitive science, neuroscience, linguistics, computer science, psychology and others, it is believed that we will be able to understand (at least partially) how brain does Natural Language Understanding (NLU) in the near future (more on NLU in Chapter

7), which in turn would result practical, more efficient and effective MT systems.

Bridging the Language Divide

Assuming that automated translation is in place for the WWW (i.e. using what we have today), it would only help people having a computer to access such information. Thus, this will only partially bridge the Language Divide. To fully bridge the Language Divide, we would need to add **Voice Internet** to it so that anyone with any phone can access any content on the Internet. With Voice Internet, the content will be translated after it is rendered. This way there would be less translation error because of the smaller size of the content. But, as already mentioned above, it is important to note that much more work is needed in machine translation to really bridge the Language Divide. So, just to reiterate, when we say bridging Language Divide, we mean bridging it using the state of the art technologies that exist today with limited translation capability that we can rely upon. Creation of new content in local languages mentioned above will significantly help bridge the Language Divide.

It is important to note that MT would also be needed to interact with the Internet as users might need to fill forms by providing input in user's language but the website could be in a different language. Thus, to fill a form in Spanish by a Chinese speaking person, the Chinese input from the Chinese user needs to be converted to Spanish before submitting the form. The same is true when a user may like to upload some content in his/her own language and then expect that to be posted in another language like English.

Multi Lingual aspect with Voice Internet

Many people (especially in Europe) speak multiple languages. For example, in Switzerland, people speak German, French and Italian. So, they usually go to websites written in these languages. Thus, it makes more sense to not use MT for these languages but use the content directly written in these preferred languages. Accordingly, the Voice Internet would need to support multi-lingual feature. A user would be asked to select a language like German or French or Italian etc and will access corresponding websites using the corresponding language. If a website supports multiple languages, then content will be displayed (or read) in the selected language. If a website does not support multiple languages then the content will be translated into the selected language using MT.

Apart from voice input, multi-lingual support would also need text input using telephone keypad or computer keyboard.

Chapter 6

Approaches to really Bridge the Digital and Language Divides—Deployment

In order to really bridge the Digital & Language Divides, we need to make sure that Voice Internet (both General Voice Internet and Custom Voice Internet) is deployed worldwide. Deploying a new technology worldwide is not simple; there are many obstacles to overcome and hence needs lots of efforts. However, because Voice Internet uses existing infrastructures and existing websites on the World Wide Web as is (i.e. no need to re-write web content in another language), the deployment process becomes simpler although there are other challenges to overcome. In this Chapter we discuss all key issues related to the deployment of Voice Internet worldwide in help bridging the Digital and Language Divides.

Easing the Deployment Process

Voice Internet can use existing infrastructure and no new infrastructure is needed. Because users would just need to make a phone call, existing mobile networks or land-line phone networks can be used. It also can use existing Internet connections—broadband, satellite, wireless or any other form of Internet connections with reasonable speed would suffice. The Internet connection is ONLY needed for the Voice Internet servers. Users would not need to have any Internet connection. User's phone becomes the browser and the phone connection acts as the Internet connection. The phone also sort of works as the computer and no computer is needed.

Besides, no new content need to be created as Voice Internet uses existing websites from the Internet or Intranet.

Similarly, existing telephone service providers can provide Voice Internet service. This is also true for existing Internet Service Providers (ISPs), Application Service Providers (ASPs) and new special service providers including Value Added Service Providers (VARs). Organizations may also decide to provide such services to meet their specific objectives. Besides, enterprises can also provide special Voice Internet services.

Thus, no new service providers are needed. However, because of the simplicity and low investment need, any small or medium company can quickly become a Voice Internet service provider and start a new business.

Because a phone is a ubiquitous device, and simple to learn and use, high level acceptance of Voice Internet by users after deployment is easier to achieve.

Challenges in Deploying Voice Internet:

Like any new technology or service, Voice Internet has some key challenges as well. These are:

(a) to ensure that cost of a phone call is low
(b) convincing phone companies (who are mainly familiar with providing phone service) to provide Internet service.
(c) creating the awareness that Internet can really be accessed by any phone and voice, without the need of a computer or a high end cell phone or a PDA.

Overcoming the Challenges:

Lowering Cost of Phone Call—

While the cost for phone calls is decreasing on a regular basis because of the competition from various providers and competition from various technologies (e.g. VoIP), it is still high and not easily affordable in several underdeveloped and developing countries due to some regulatory issues and other factors. There are multiple ways to bring the cost down to a much more affordable level when users call for Voice Internet service. For example, governments can provide some regulatory mechanisms to use low cost phone call when certain specific numbers are called that would provide access to a Voice Internet service. Governments can also subsidize the rate or provide it free for certain services like e-Gov. or e-Learning.

Service providers (especially phone companies) can provide very low phone charge when a Voice Internet service is called as phone companies would not get such additional revenue anyway without the Voice Internet service. So, they can afford to provide low cost rate as they will still have good new additional revenue with high ROI (Return on Investment).

World bodies like UN, ITU, WSIS can also make policy recommendations to enforce special rates and tariff when phone calls are used to access Voice Internet as it would help easy access to both general information, and various key specific information including education, health, and farming which in turn will help economic, social, cultural and other developments and thus help achieve the MDGs (Millennium Development Goals).

Convincing Phone Companies & other Service Providers—

As already mentioned, Voice Internet service can be provided by phone companies—Voice Internet is a good marriage between the telephone and the Internet. However, it is not always easy to convince a phone provider to provide Voice Internet service as phone companies are not usually familiar with Internet services and hence are not set up for such services from infrastructure, operational, marketing and other business standpoints. ISPs are mainly focused on providing Internet using a computer. So, they usually do not think of potential users who would not use a computer. In some cases they take this as a kind of threat as they believe it might convince some people not to buy and use a computer. Such ISPs are not set up for such a service from infrastructure, operational, marketing and other business standpoints. This situation is, however, changing fast, especially for some forward looking service providers who see the value and understand how they can clearly differentiate them from competitors.

A practical way to work with ISPs and phone companies is to look for such forward looking service provider companies with good vision.

However, it might not be easy to find such forward looking service provider companies. A better alternative is to find new forward looking service provider like companies who are really looking for some new value added services, especially with killer applications. Such startup minded forwarding looking companies try hard to make such new services successful. The key problem is that they may not have good service, operations, marketing and business infrastructure. However, these can easily be overcome as these can be learned easily or outsourced easily.

Making Voice Internet available in all Internet Cafés, schools and key public places are also good ways of fast deployment and increased usage. Government and other welfare type organizations (elderly, blind, disabled, . . .) can also directly deploy Voice Internet services.

In fact, Voice Internet is already deployed using all these approaches in several countries.

Creating the Awareness—

A good Private-Public partnership can help awareness fast. Many global, regional and local organizations including United Nations, World Bank, ITU, USAID, Lions Club, Rotary Club, NGOs and many others whose key objective is to bridge the Digital Divide, can play a major role in publicity, promotion, mobilizing and funding as appropriate to deploy such services worldwide. Some of these organizations, especially, United Nations, World Bank, ITU can formulate strong policies to make Voice Internet available at all Internet Café and Internet Kiosks.

Education & Training:

Education & Training is another very important key element. People at the bottom of the pyramid have heard about the Internet in radios, TVs, news papers and magazines. But they are not comfortable in learning and using it as they do not know what exactly Internet is, how Internet works etc. Thus, we would need to provide some important training on the Internet, Voice Internet and how to use it. Such program needs to be publicized well. There are usually established computer training centers in many countries. Such centers would be a good place to teach Voice Internet.

To rapidly grow number of users, various promotional programs as well as various favorite applications need to be developed and deployed. A few examples are free access to most needed information like News Headlines, Weather Forecast, directory assistance, e-Services (including e-Gov, e-Learning, e-Health, e-Agriculture, e-Commerce), popular blogging sites, most popular websites and the like. Among these, **four e-Services (e-Gov, e-Learning, e-Health and e-Agriculture)** need special attention as their deployment can also **expedite the Voice Internet adoption process.** The **e-Learning, e-Agriculture or e-Farming and e-Commerce, in addition, can significantly help improve efficiency (lowering cost), and also help in innovation & entrepreneurship.** Hence, brief descriptions on e-Gov, e-Learning and e-Health are provided below. And detailed descriptions on **education and e-Learning,** along with **innovation & entrepreneurship** are provided in Chapter 8. The impact on **Economic, Social, Cultural and other developments** are also very important, and hence are emphasized in Chapter 8.

e-Gov Applications—an imperative

e-Governance is the computerization and automation of common administrative processes (including government processes) to ensure more transparency, efficiency and service orientation using ICT and electronic media. Thus, the goal of e-Governance is to lowering costs, improving efficiency and generally providing better services to citizens.

e-Governance is improving the lives of billions of people worldwide and is integrating government services in a way never seen before. Linux (an open-source version of the UNIX operating system Ref # [LinkUnix]) with its low cost, high security and open standards is rapidly becoming the driving force behind this revolution.

It is important to further clarify the benefits of e-Governance with some real examples to appreciate the need of e-Governance.

A. Make Government services hassle-free, faster, cheaper, more inclusive and "at citizens doorsteps".
B. Bring efficiency, effectiveness, transparency and accountability to administration.
C. Enable people's voice in decision making (as people can directly interact electronically)
D. Minimize corruption (as electronic processing eliminates/automates major steps for possible corruption)

A few Examples:

1. *Accessing Public Records seamlessly in an automated way*—citizens will be able to access public records (like Land related forms, Birth Certificates, University Admission forms and the like), fill necessary forms and submit them automatically on their own. Several steps of the Government existing processes in this regard will be automated saving huge costs, improving efficiency and with a great customer service.
2. *Bill Payment*—users will be able to pay various bills like electric bill, water bill, gas bill without staying in a long line.
3. *E-procurement*—Government will be able to make its procurement process very effective by automating it using ICT.
4. *Job service*—various job related services can be automated making it very useful and simple for users.
5. *Government administrative processes* (file transfer, entering data in files, analyzing comments, sharing files to all involved etc) will be very simplified.

Thus, the need for e-Gov is very clear. It is important to note that because of the large Digital Divide, high population density, many people under the poverty line and the like, the need for e-Gov, in general, is more prominent in the developing and underdeveloped countries. But there are large Digital Divides in some sections of population in the developed countries as well (e.g. in U.S. there is a large Digital Divide in Native Indians as well as in rural areas). So, the need for e-Gov can also be prominent for some section of people in developed countries.

However, e-Gov with traditional methods would still require to have a computer or a similar device. This is a critical issue for many people at the base of the pyramid because of four main reasons:

1. *affordability,*
2. *difficult to learn how to use a computer,*
3. *difficult to use a computer (or a similar device) and*
4. *illiteracy*

as already mentioned under the limitations of existing approaches to access the Internet. This is also true for Internet access using all small screen based devices.

#2 to #4 cause fear or discomfort in using a computer. This is reflected in many applications accessed by computer including e-Gov applications. The adoption rate for using such applications has been low.

As already mentioned, it is important to note that use of e-Gov applications are more important for base of the Pyramid people as they would need more help from the government. Rich people are usually educated, have computers and can easily access government applications when needed. In fact, although they can access such applications, their need to access such applications is far less than those at the base of the pyramid. Why? Well, poor or people at the base of the pyramid need to find out what kind of help they can get from the Government. A farmer may get some subsidy or loan. A jobless person would need to apply for a job. On the other hand, a rich or financially solvent person would not need such help. Rather government would need help from rich people; in many cases rich people and companies help government events using various forms of sponsorship to do business with the Government In such cases, usually government will contact such companies using various communication means including phone call or email or possibly using an e-Gov application. Companies may do the same. But, clearly, today the use of e-Gov applications is very limited as base of the pyramid people do not have access to it whereas they are the one who would need to access it because of the reasons explained above.

This is where **Voice Internet technology** *makes a big difference as it is very affordable, does not require any literacy and very easy to learn & use. Accordingly,*

Voice Internet can bring the benefits of e-Gov to many more people as number of phones far outstrips the number of computers (computers represent only 14% of total phone population as there are 550million connected computers versus over 5 billion total phones in the world as already mentioned).

e-Learning Application—an imperative

With growing needs for education around the world, many organizations including various educational institutions (universities, colleges, high schools, vocational institutes, various other training centers and the like), organizations, NGOs and Governments have started showing strong emphasis on distance learning or e-Learning.

The need for education is based on various factors—e.g. creating skilled work force for economic, social, cultural and other developments; increased peace by minimizing terrorism; gaining competitive edge, and earning global respect. All such factors are equally applicable for e-Learning. Because of the large Digital Divide, high population density, many people under the poverty line and the like, e-Learning need is more prominent in the developing and underdeveloped countries. But there are large Digital Divides in some sections of population in the developed countries as well (e.g. in U.S. there is a large Digital Divide in Native Indians as well as in rural areas). So, e-Learning is needed for all countries.

However, e-Learning with traditional methods would still require to have a computer or a similar device. This is a critical issue for many people at the base of the pyramid because of four main reasons: affordability, difficult to learn how to use a computer, difficult to use a computer and illiteracy.

This is where Voice Internet technology makes a big difference as it is very affordable, does not require any literacy and very easy to learn & use. Accordingly, Voice Internet can bring the benefits of e-Learning to much more people as number of phone far outstrips the number of computers.

Key Benefits

- *Increased ROI*
- *Greater level of customer satisfaction*

- *Consistent service through automation*
- *Shorter call times through easy navigation and elimination of hold time as compared to a human operator or a DTMF system.*
- *Reduction in operational cost through automation and shorter call times*
- *Better service through better call handling capacity and lesser dropped calls.*
- *Easy access to other Internet services (e.g. after finishing e-Learning, a users can go to email, search or shopping application). netECHO basically makes it a web based IVR so that user can easily access all web related features and applications.*

e-Health Application—an imperative

With growing needs for better health around the world, many organizations including various NGOs and Governments have started showing strong emphasis on e-Health.

The need for better health is based on various factors—e.g. better productivity from the workforce, lower cost for the health systems (as there would be less health problems), lower death rate, lower number of diseases and happier society. All such factors are equally applicable for e-Health. Because of the large Digital Divide, high population density, many people under the poverty line and the like, e-Health need is more prominent in the developing and underdeveloped countries. But there are large Digital Divides in some sections of population in the developed countries as well (e.g. in U.S. there is a large Digital Divide in Native Indians as well as in rural areas). So, e-Health is needed for all countries.

However, e-Health with traditional methods would still require to have a computer or a similar device. This is a critical issue for many people at the base of the pyramid because of four main reasons: affordability, difficult to learn how to use a computer or complex devices, difficult to use a computer and illiteracy.

This is where Voice Internet technology makes a big difference as it is very affordable, does not require any literacy and very easy to learn & use. Accordingly, Voice Internet can bring the benefits of e-Health to much more people as number of phone far outstrips the number of computers as explained above.

With voice Health or v-Health, user would be able to learn common things about health from a Health Portal (including information on AIDS, Swine Flu and the like), access patient records, order prescription, communicate with doctors and more.

Chapter 7

Voice Internet—an enabling technology for Several New Products and Services

Voice Internet is the best way to provide Internet to maximum number of people in the world today considering cost, usability and ability to easily learn. The reasons are clear—a phone, the most ubiquitous device, is much cheaper and easier to learn and use. Voice and hearing are the two most natural user interfaces, and also enable a mobile person to access and enjoy the Internet in an eyes busy-hands busy situation (like while driving or walking).

However, there are cases where a visual display can also help a lot (e.g. viewing a picture or a table of data). Also, providing Internet through other ubiquitous devices like a TV and Radio would extend the accessibility of the Internet to many more people, especially, in the developing and underdeveloped world. For a hearing impaired person, a visual display device like a TV, PDA or phone would be more preferable. As discussed in Chapter 3, available Internet content on mobile phone with small screen is very limited as the content need to be re-written with another language like WML, CHTML or the like. Re-writing such content is impractical as there are over 3 billion websites and so it would be cost prohibitive. Besides, navigation will be very difficult, if not impossible, as re-writing into several small pages to fit into the screen would create too many pages, making it difficult to navigate. Fortunately, the "rendering technology" of the Voice Internet described in the previous chapters, is an **enabling**

technology as it can provide Internet content from the World Wide Web (WWW) or from Intranet on any

a) mobile phone screen at ease and without the need for any re-writing of website with another language,
b) television screen at ease,
c) radio
   and more.

In this Chapter I will describe all such new media/devices that extend the Internet to much more people through TV, radio, any phone with display screen, PDA, simple or regular computer, and the like in a **very easy, usable and affordable way**. Some of such solutions also enable many more people to access a computer. These new media/devices include **MicroBrowser** (allowing any website content to be automatically displayed on any cell phone or PDA screen at ease), **TV Browser** (allowing to easily view and navigate websites using a regular TV), **Radio Browser** (allowing listening to the Internet using a radio), **Voice Computer** (allowing a user to store, edit and manipulates file etc. on a server computer), **netTalk** (allowing VoIP call using no broadband phone or no broadband connection), and more [Courtesy: InternetSpeech, Inc].

Rendering to a new medium—MicroBrowser

As we all know, the growth of cell phone has been phenomenal. The main usage of cell phone as of today is for talking and listening. That is the key reason we have emphasized on the Voice Internet using any phone including cell phone. The visual (data) usage has been very limited (about 15% of world cell phones have display screen for Internet browsing and not all of them are used for Internet access; in other words, cell phone based Internet access represent a fraction of this 15% phones having display screen). The key reasons for such low usage are

(a) limited content that are re-written (few thousand sites on Wireless web versus over 3 billion sites on WWW) with another language suitable for viewing on small screen

(b) difficulty in navigation as the navigation tree may be too long when there are many small pages on a website

(c) high data cost for a data package

The trend shows that data usage is increasing, especially with PDA-like cell phone (like iPhone) but not on non PDA like cell phones (the regular cell phones) which represent over 85% of over 4.2 billion cell phones that exist today. So, if nothing major is changed, the usage for viewing is not expected to rise much (iPhone is not affordable for many, and will still not be affordable by many even if the price will go down on a regular basis as Apple and similar companies business model will not be attractive if the price becomes too low). On the other hand, if somehow, content from the Internet (WWW) and Intranet can be displayed at ease on any cell phone screen with easy navigation and at low cost, it is very logical to say that Internet access through cell phone will increase rapidly. Fortunately, this can be done using the Voice Internet "rendering technology".

The two key media for rendering large content into short content are

(a) Audio using any phone (as in Voice Internet) and

(b) Visual display screen using a cell phone screen or PDA.

It is important to note that the Internet was designed with visual access in a large screen in mind. So, all the information is laid out that attract our eyes on a sizeable screen (like in a computer) but not attract our ears or eyes when displayed on a small screen—cell phone or PDA.

There is a good synergy between the two modes mentioned in (a) and (b) from rendering standpoint. Both needs small amount of meaningful information at a time that can be heard or viewed at ease with easy navigation. This is achieved by using the Page Highlights feature and finding relevant content (on the new page arrived after selecting a Highlight), "column at a time" like we do when we read a news paper or website, as described in Chapter 4.

A column of text information can be converted to audio that can be heard with ease. The rate of hearing i.e. content delivery can be controlled to suit user's needs. The selection of a website, Page Highlight, speed of hearing etc can be all done by Voice Commands. These are the key features of the Voice Internet i.e. basically talking and listening to the Internet as described in Chapters 3 & 4.

The same column of rendered text can be displayed on a small screen that can be viewed at ease as a small screen can easily display a column of texts, but not a whole page. The content are then automatically scrolled using desired speed if it is also heard in audio (i.e. if audio is turned on). If audio is turned off, then auto scrolling will be off and user will scroll vertically at user's choice. This is what results a MicroBrowser or "true" wireless Internet accessibility, viewing & navigation that do not need any re-writing of the website, and present content at ease in a meaningful way on a cell phone or PDA screen. Because, rendering does data mining i.e. finds desired data from the page as opposed to re-writing the page in several small tiny pages, the navigation becomes much easier and practical. Thus, a MicroBrowser enables anyone to view and navigate any website at ease. It also enables a PDA user to get to any desired content without manually scrolling and trying to figuring out what's on the whole page. Apart from accessing desired content (including multi-media content), MicroBrowser allows one to fill various types of forms and complete online transactions. This way **existing wireless web automatically get extended to the World Wide Web (WWW) i.e. whole WWW becomes available on any cell phone screen at ease with easy navigation.**

It is important to note that vertically scrolling a column of text is not unnatural as we do the same in a computer for some websites. This is different than vertically scrolling the content of a whole page as done in some mobile browsers like Opera. When scrolling a column of texts in a MicroBrowser, the story in the column does not usually change which is not the case when scrolling the content of the whole page.

Easing Navigation

A MicroBrowser digs the content in real time, avoiding long navigation trees if the content were re-written with another language (like in a WAP) into several small pages. As an example, let's consider a portal website like Yahoo. To represent complete WWW Yahoo website in a WAP website, there would be many small pages in WML. If the website has 100 pages on WWW and we need to break these 100 pages into, say 1000 small pages, then to navigate to 999th page would take a long tree of selection process; thus making it almost impossible to use. This is the reason a WML version of a website uses only a fraction of the website content on WWW. MicroBrowser does not limit this content viewing as it goes and digs the desired content and makes the navigation simple by using only a few steps to get to the desired content. **Thus, a MicroBrowser really solves the Wireless Internet problem by allowing complete access to all pages and websites without any re-writing of website and with easy navigation and rendering.**

Rendering to a new medium—SMS Browser

SMS Browser allows to view any Website content on any cell Phone or PDA screen comfortably based on SMS based communication. It is similar to displaying email content in a mobile phone. SMS Browser works with World Wide Web i.e. no re-writing of the web site in another language like WML is needed. Thus, SMS Browser will enable to access any website on the WWW on any cell phone or PDA. Users can do Surfing, Searching, Email, e-Commerce and more by interacting with the Internet using SMS messaging.

Rendering to a new medium—TV Browser

It is clear that using existing basic communication devices (like a simple phone), Internet access devices (computers, PDAs, mobile phones), and enabling Television/radios to allow bi-directional communication, would significantly enable advancement of social interaction of many people.

So, the next natural question is "what devices mentioned above are readily available, easy to learn, easy to use, affordable, and effective to interact?" The simple answer is "simple phone, TV and radio" [It is important to note that more capable and complex mobile phones and PDAs automatically converted (via "MicroBrowser" as described above) to act as a simple phone falls under this category]. So, if we can provide Internet Access and Interaction through such devices then we will achieve our objectives of Bridging the Digital and Language Divides in one of the best possible ways. We already have covered access through phones using audio and visual forms. Let's take a look in using TV for similar access.

Rendering will enable a TV to be converted into a nice and easy-to-use Internet access device. The existing set-top box based Internet Access using a TV is difficult for many people as they would need to interface and navigate through a complex interface. A rendered interface to a TV (via a smarter set-top box using Voice Internet rendering), will make the interface to the Internet much simpler (similar to accessing via a MicroBrowser as described above), allowing very user friendly, easy to learn and easy to use way to experience the Internet on a TV. For example, when a user select a website, only Highlights of the Home page (usually 3 at a time) will be displayed on the screen or played in the speaker. User then will select a Highlight and then the selected story will be displayed on the screen. This is very similar to reading (or listening to) a news paper. Through TV Remote Control, user will be able to go to any website, navigate to any page and easily view and listen desired rendered content. A TV Browser basically converts the Internet into News Paper pages. TV Browser is also easier to learn and use, and more effective than viewing on a cell phone screen using a MicroBrowser.

Rendering to a new medium—Radio Browser

Listening and interacting to the Internet using a radio will be very user friendly and easy to use if content can be rendered in audio with easy navigation. This is very similar to Voice Internet using any phone as you will be listening and interacting with the Internet using a radio instead of a phone. However, it will be easier to hear as radio has a good speaker. To ensure that users will be able to interact with the Internet and hence go to different websites or search various words, interaction will be done either through an improved radio with a set-top box suitable for a radio.

Alternatively, it might be better to use a TV Browser and then use another form of output from the TV Browser that would act like transmitting through a local radio transmitter. The user can then use a simple radio receiver to tune the website to listen. The radio receiver will have some enhancement to support bi-directional capability so that user can type a website or say a website. The TV remote (or radio receiver remote control) will have such simple interface for interaction.

Rendering to a new medium—Tablet PC

Tablet PC is a simple PC without a complex keyboard. Some Tablet PC dos not have keyboard or mouse; only a 3-4 hard buttons and some soft buttons. Apple's iPad can be grouped under Tablet PC.

Tablet PC Browser allows a Tablet PC to support easy rendering, navigation, interaction, etc. The same applies for a PC Browser (see below for details). For many users, using an Internet Browser (like Internet Explorer, Mozilla) is not straight forward. Besides, using Windows or other operating system is difficult for many people. A rendering interface to a Tablet PC, will make the interface to a computer much simpler, allowing a very user friendly, easy to learn and easy to use way to experience the Internet or files in a computer.

Rendering to a new medium—Voice Computer

Computers are great as we all know. However, many people are fearful about learning and using a computer. For many people, interacting with a computer via its operating system is a daunting task. The same is true when one tries to interact with an Internet Browser.

Voice Internet rendering engine can be used to render a computer's display screen so that a user can perform most of the computer interface over any phone.

Thus, it provides capability to store desired web content, search for the previously stored content, moving files, editing files, use of limited commands etc using any phone. Basically, each user has a virtual computer on a server with allocated space. Thus, a user can call a phone number and choose a particular web site to store the data in a file on the server computer, retrieve that file and make edits at a later time, search a particular file(s) in a pre-allocated directory/sub-directory allocated for the user. This is basically having an online computer with good accessibility by using a simple phone and using user's voice.

Thus, Voice Computer will extend many benefits of a computer to a much larger population who do not have a computer, can't afford to buy a computer, or have difficulty in learning and using a computer. With a Voice Computer, users will be able to get a computer via a phone and perform all basic functions.

A variation of a Voice Computer is a Virtual Computer that can be accessed visually using a mobile phone with display screen. This will allow a mobile phone user to view directories, edit files, send resume etc using a cell phone and a virtual computer in a server.

Rendering to a new medium—netTalk: VoIP call using a simple phone

VoIP call using a simple phone is basically connecting people over the Internet using any phone. An example is netTalk from InternetSpeech. It **uses InternetSpeech Patented** Voice Internet technology, neteCHO®, to connect a user to the Internet using any telephone. While connected on the Internet, netTalk allows a user to connect to a VoIP calling solution (e.g. SkypeOut). This is done by using neteCHO's automated "rendering" feature. Such feature allows netECHO to find right hooks to the VoIP application and then controlling the necessary hooks to complete and maintain the VoIP call. netECHO also converts caller and recipient's Voice into correct audio files that can be played over any telephone. Automatic rendering of correct "forms" on the web application allows smooth call transformation from a PSTN call to VoIP call, and finally completing the call to any phone including a POTS (plain old telephone service) telephone. Thus, a person with an old simple telephone (or using any phone) can talk to another person in U.S. or any country in the world where VoIP is supported with PSTN (or any phone) at a much lower cost.

netTalk brings computer based VoIP call to everyone with a simple phone, using netECHO® (Fig. 7.1).

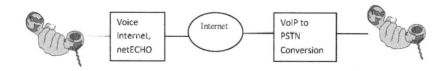

Fig. 7.1: netTalk enables very low cost telecommunication using netECHO®Voice Internet. VoIP call and VoIP to PSTN conversion are done by 3rd party companies like Skype, Vonage, Google, . . .

Moving Existing IVRs (Interactive Voice Response System) to Web Based IVR

Existing IVR systems are stand alone systems and are not connected to the corresponding web based applications. Any change in the application (for example on the web site) needs to be incorporated separately in the IVR systems. This causes higher cost to develop and maintain a standalone IVR system.

Existing IVR systems sometimes include a small fraction of the corresponding web based applications. For example, one can do some banking using a bank IVR system. But one can do much more using web based banking application. Using Voice Internet rendering engine, any web based application can be Voice Enabled automatically by making some small changes in the front end dialogue, thus significantly lowering the cost of development & maintenance. The same web application can be accessed using a computer or using any phone. This is basically converting all stand alone IVRs to web-based IVRs.

Besides, the web based IVR applications will be much more flexible. For example, today's applications are multi-faceted in nature. For example, if one makes an air line ticket reservation, he/she would possibly like to make a hotel reservation and / or a car rental reservation. A web based IVR can seamlessly handle such requests whereas with existing approaches one would have to call three separate IVR systems.

It is important to note that web based IVR is not same as Custom Voice Internet, although there are some similarities. Custom Voice Internet usually focus on one application whereas web based IVR brings whole Internet and associated applications to any phone.

Making Computers Usable By Many More People

Many people who are not familiar with computers find it difficult to learn how to use a computer. Many others find it difficult to use because of complex user interface through the Operating System, complex keyboard, Graphical User Interface (GUI), needs to keep on learning new things like adware, spyware, virus control, security options in using the Internet, navigating through the Internet, finding appropriate desired content and the like.

Data from several sources show that many new users from the Digital Divide are fearful about learning how to use a computer and fearful about learning and using the Internet. Many elderly and blind people also find it difficult to learn how to use a computer. Many elderly and blind people who already learned how to use it and have been using it for a long time also find it difficult to keep on learning new stuff on a regular basis as well as using it.

For such people, fixing a computer after infected by some very harmful virus is a nightmare and expensive task. Many people would prefer to have some technician come home (as opposed to getting help over the phone) in spite of high cost to fix such problems.

A simple solution to the difficulty in using a of computer is to use key features of Voice Internet in a computer so that users can enjoy the simplicity of using voice and audio, "soft" telephone keypad (i.e. using a touch tone phone displayed on a computer screen) and automated rendering and navigation. For example, by adding Voice Internet, will make Internet experience much easier as one would be able to automatically get highlights of a page, select it by voice and then automatically getting the desire content displayed on the screen or playing it by a media player. Similarly, a user would be able to use simple commands to do edits, manipulate files etc without any need to learn key features of a keyboard or learning how to use series of steps using GUI.

Voice Internet in a computer simply makes it a Very Simple Computer and Voice Internet in a Simple Computer makes it even more simple and easy to use by many more people.

Question and Answer System

It is very clear that we would need to provide all the key benefits of the Information Age to the base of the Pyramid people in a very simple and easy to learn and easy to use way. This is even more so since many people at the base of the Pyramid are illiterate. Accordingly, we would need to make sure that only precise answers are provided to their questions. Thus, if they are searching for a word(s), it will be almost meaningless to provide all the results based on today's string based search engines.

We also would need to make sure that they can ask their questions in a natural way using their natural language.

This implies that we would need a more advanced Intelligent Agent (IA) that can understand natural language, get the desired content from various sources, assemble the appropriate content and then deliver the desired content in a simple natural way. This, of course, is a daunting task as Natural Language Understanding problem is not solved yet (as mentioned in Chapter 5), a solution to get the desired content and assemble them in a succinct manner is not possible yet when it is unconstrained i.e. when we would like to do it for any sentence and any topic. So, we may need to wait for a long time before we can get a general Q&A system.

However, the problem can be tackled reasonably well when we consider some specific domain. And that itself would be good for many existing problems—e.g. a Q&A system for some key aspects of Farming is realizable. Thus, Voice Internet, Natural Language Understanding and associated technologies show strong promise to develop "Digital Aladdin's Lamp" (a simple device that would provide answers to most common questions asked verbally, starting with some specific domains) that Yunus ([Yunus2007], [Fortune2008]) and others have envisioned.

Need for Natural Language Understanding

Clearly, to make a good Q&A System for any domain, we would need to solve NLU problem, automated reliable Language Translation problem, generating the summary of a story problem and the like. As mentioned in Chapter 5, NLU is a very complex problem and it is strongly believed that we would need to use Brain-Like and bio-inspired algorithms to effectively solve the NLU problem.

The success of traditional algorithms / methods (including **Evolutionary Computing/Computational Intelligence**) to address this complex NLU problem has been very limited. Continuing the use of traditional methods and their various combinations with super fast machines does not seem to yield real practical solutions to this and similar complex problems. On the other hand, much slowly running human brain processors can solve such problems at ease in real time.

Based on many studies, I strongly believe that we will have much better success to solve such complex problems by **learning from human brain**. Although ANN (Artificial Neural Networks) is claimed to be based on the computational model in neurons in human brain, there is a large gap between ANN (as we know today) and how neurons really work in our brain (especially at system level)—a good example is the level of feedback connections in ANN versus in human brain neural system. Another good example is the effect of the inputs and environment on the neural behavior /structure in human brain neural system which is not usually considered in ANN. Functional genomics and gene expression also plays important role in biological neural system—these are not included in today's ANN. Minimizing the gap between ANN and biological neural system (especially neural system in human brain) by better understanding how human brain works (even partially) and taking as much information as we can to today's ANN, can help solve (or partially solve) NLU and similar other open problems like machine vision, reasoning and perception.

We would need to work with related **multi-disciplinary** fields including Cognitive Science, Neuroscience, and Biological Science/Life Science (especially focusing on **human brain** functional aspects). The key work in this regard seem to have **TWO broad approaches**:

a. Consider developing more capable and robust ANN architecture / system by better understanding and using various key approaches in human brain including Development System (from zygot to full brain development), Cellular System, Neural System and Behavioral System.

b. Better understand how human brain works & learns, especially, the language understanding / processing (using Neo cortex), environmental interaction, collective systems and the components mentioned in (a) above. And then develop algorithms to solve key problems at hand.

Both of these approaches are needed as #a may be too complex to achieve but can produce results otherwise unattainable, and #b can make it easier to understand and develop algorithms providing practical solutions to the problems at hand.

By working with multi-disciplinary teams and using state of the art approaches to detect and monitor key brain activities, it is hoped that we will have reasonable understanding how key functionalities, especially, how NLU works in human brain in the near future.

PART THREE

Towards a New World
of Prosperity

Chapter 8

What's next after the Digital and Language Divides are Bridged from Connectivity Standpoint?

"Life is pretty simple: You do some stuff. Most fails. Some works. You do more of what works. If it works big, others quickly copy it. Then you do something else. The trick is the doing something else"—Leonardo Da Vinci

Let's assume that together with conventional methods of using computers, PDAs, cell phones, and the proposed method of Voice Internet, the Digital and Language Divides are really bridged from connection standpoint. Now what? Well, the benefits of getting into the Internet need to be utilized properly to really help meet basic needs including food, shelter, education, communication, health, business and economy. To really bridge the Digital Divide, we would need to address the other key factors:

*u**tilize the access to information to knowledge, use knowledge to drive innovation & entrepreneurship to finally drive the development. Education is a key component to develop knowledge from the information. It is also a key component for innovation and entrepreneurship.***

Thus, education is a very important key element. To stimulate real economic growth, "education" needs to be highly emphasized and targeted, especially with **"creativity"**, **"productivity"** and **"resource"** creation in mind. Creativity will in turn **drive innovation, entrepreneurship,**

productivity (and even resources—like discovering new oil reserve, alternate energy . . .) resulting successful business entities which in turn will create jobs and **drive economy reducing rich-poor gap**. In a nut shell, the key idea is to use the benefits of getting to the Internet to create valuable resources.

Fostering Education:

The importance of education has been growing since human civilization. It is the cornerstone for growth and ensures sustainable development. Unfortunately, the education systems in the underdeveloped and developing countries, in general, are farther behind than the educational systems in developed countries. Many of the world's children receive no formal education or a sub-standard education. Many lack books, materials and have no or little communication with the wider world. This is also true to some extent within a rich country where some good level of Digital Divide exists in the suburb or in some races (e.g. in U.S, Alaskan and Native Indians do not have a good education system and they usually do not participate in the advanced education system that U.S has). The course curricula is based on old method of traditional non digital books, old text books and subjects/courses, lecture method with writing on blackboards, no lecture notes, limited homework mainly from the text book and the like.

So, in fostering education there are quite a few issues that would need to be addressed. A few important ones are:

1. improved courses.
2. teaching/lecturing methods.
3. access to library and digital information sources including, the Internet.
4. management of college/university system using computers to improve efficiency and accuracy.
5. much more frequent update of course curricula by following the same from rich education system as well ensuring that local needs are properly met.
6. introducing distance learning.
7. formal courses to teach the teachers with new courses and methods.

8. allowing students to use Internet at home to help improve their study, solving home works, writing reports and the like.
9. Special emphasis on "**informal education**" as many people at the base of the pyramid cannot afford to go to school for a long time to get a formal degree.
10. ensure that education is also closely related to job needs and growth.
11. ensure that education also strongly focus on **entrepreneurship and innovation.**
12. strong emphasis on immediate, short term and long term needs

Fostering Innovation:

Education is great and essential but not sufficient to have great impact. E.g. even after everybody is well educated, most possibly there will be more job seekers than number of jobs. So, education itself will not solve the ultimate goal of great economic development.

Innovation is a very important element to apply education in a manner it is impactful in solving some key problems in more efficient ways, and thus, help many people and in turn help economic growth. Innovation does not need to be at high level—it can be at all levels. So, there is no need to think that only certain highly educated people can do innovation. In fact, many illiterate people can be very innovative in solving their key problems. This is why we would need to emphasize on both formal and informal education as many people at the base of the Pyramid can become innovative faster using informal education.

Similarly, higher education is key for innovation at high level. Thus, graduate studies in key subject areas including science, engineering, medicine, and business are very important. A pure technical innovation may not be effective in producing good results unless there are also innovation in marketing, sales and business development.

Innovation needs to be in almost everything including improving various types of existing systems (transportation, communication, business processes, . . .), automating various processes (economic, social, . . .), coming up with new product or business ideas (in the local, regional or global contexts), and research. Thus, we would need to make innovation as part of our culture.

Fostering Entrepreneurship:

Innovation & Education alone cannot really make things happen unless innovations are implemented using a sound business model. Thus fostering "entrepreneurship" using innovation is the key to take full advantage of innovation—developing products and services, deploying them to the users, ensuring that such products and services are beneficial to the users & society, and thus helping social, economic, cultural and other developments. These will also help monetize the innovation. Like innovation, entrepreneurship should also be at all levels.

A Few Examples of Innovation and Entrepreneurship:

Grameen Bank: A creative business idea to lend money to the poor and ensure repayment by entrepreneurial ideas of the borrowers. Borrowers would need to use the money to do some business to earn enough to return the money and feed them as well. Most borrowers did not have any education but because of their creativity and efforts they became successful. Of course, original idea came from a well known economist Nobel Laureate Muhammad Yunus who got the Nobel Peace prize in 2006.

Another good example is **software outsourcing** in India. In this case the education was more formal and targeted as the country figured out (using both local and expatriate talents) that information technology will be an important key in this information age. Hence, a very good skill set was developed by most leading institutions which was utilized properly by innovators and entrepreneurs.

Another example is the innovation and entrepreneurship driven businesses in **Silicon Valley**, California which has dramatically changed the world and world economy. This is the key reason why US has been leading so long and continue to do so for a while. It is also important to note that no nation can continue to lead forever—thus there are opportunities for everyone.

These examples show that education, innovation, creativity, productivity and resources are important keys for initiating as well as sustaining economic growth. In general, the level of innovation / creativity has more influence to the level of the economic growth. So, innovation is very key at all levels of economic development. Without innovation we would be still hunting to meet our daily food needs.

Driving Education, Innovation and Entrepreneurship

Now that we have recognized and discussed the importance of education, innovation and entrepreneurship, the next natural question is "how should we drive these to achieve the desired goals?" Before answering that, let's briefly see what various organizations have been doing in this regard, where we are today and how to move forward.

The UN, many governments, NGOs and other organizations recognized the need to improve the education worldwide to ensure real global development. The initiatives taken by the UN are worth describing in more details. The UN initiated a few very good programs including Global Alliance for ICT and Development (GAID) [GaidICT2007], "ICT for Education", and GeSCI (The Global e-Schools and Communities Initiatives) [Bracey2005]. GeSCI was established in 2004. In a statement, the then UN Secretary General Kofi Annan said "The Global e-Schools and Communities Initiatives matches the power of ICT with educational need, and has the potential not only to improve education, but also to empower people, strengthen governance, open up new markets and galvanizing our efforts to achieve the Millennium Development Goals". These initiatives have already resulted impressive results in some underdeveloped & developing countries. The UN initiatives focuses on connectivity, achieving universal primary education, gender equality and creating private-public partnerships to realize potential of ICT for development. The GAID has extended this further to include entrepreneurship and innovation. The long term objectives of GAID are provided below:

1. Mainstreaming the global ICT agenda into the broader United Nations development agenda.
2. Bringing together key organizations and other stakeholders involved in ICT for development to enhance their collaboration

and effectiveness for achieving the internationally agreed development goals.

3. Raising awareness of policy makers on ICTD policy issues.
4. Facilitating identification of technological solutions for specific development needs and goals launching of pertinent partnerships.
5. Promoting creation of an enabling environment and innovative business models for pro-poor investment, innovation & entrepreneurship and growth and for empowering people living in poverty and other marginalized communities, and
6. providing the Secretary-General with advice on ICTD related issues.

These are very good goals to really start making noticeable and sizeable development in the underdeveloped & developing countries and the whole world as well. The ideas and recommendations made in the next two chapters are, in general, along the same line of these objectives. However, I have **emphasized** (in this and the following two chapters) on the **missing components, alternative solutions, more details and much stronger emphasis on the entrepreneurship and innovation** with some good business models to really make the development efforts successful with local, regional and Global development in mind. Thus, proposed approaches will enable all the stakeholders (including UN) to work even more closely and effectively to not only **implement the UN objectives but go beyond to use poor's brain for global development.**

Computers, simple computers and other similar devices would provide connectivity as well as implement all these key issues mentioned above. But again when such a device is not available (which of course will remain the case for many people, especially in the underdeveloped and developing countries), **Voice Internet** would become a very handy and effective tool. For example, a student would be able to access the Internet from home using any phone to help in solving the homeworks, writing reports etc. Many students would be able to do some of these works when they ride on the bus to get to their home. Teachers who would have difficulty in learning how to use a computer would be highly benefited from Voice Internet. Similarly, many teachers or students who are not comfortable in learning how to use a computer or a computer is not available to them, would be highly benefited.

In this globalized world, rural students would need to compete with urban students, students in an underdeveloped country would need to compete with students in a developed country to really move up from where they are. Even though many schools now have computers, when students go home, many of them yet do not have any computers. So, to do their home works or reports, they either would need to call someone who has a computer and Internet access or go to a nearby library which may be closed or there may not be a library nearby. And many schools even do not have any computers yet—so teachers in such schools cannot even assign home works or reports that are comparable to a school in a developed country. Voice Internet can significantly help in such situations as students would be able to access the Internet at schools, at their homes and also while they are going back to home or going to schools assuming that they would have a mobile phone which is the case for many students.

Apart from doing home works, reports or research, students would also need to learn by taking courses remotely. Thus, the need for distance learning is growing fast in developed countries. The importance of the distance learning would be even more important for the underdeveloped & developing countries as there may not be enough number of schools in some rural areas, many cannot afford to attend beyond primary education as it is not free in many countries, and many are too busy in getting some income to feed themselves and do not have time to go to school for education. Voice Internet would be ideal for such people as most of them would not even have any computers. Besides, Voice Internet will resolve or ease the other problems just mentioned. Distance learning is a great way for the under developed & developing countries to get exposed to the advanced courses from the developed countries. Voice Internet will enable many more people from the underdeveloped & developing countries to enjoy such advanced courses from the developed countries.

Besides, Voice Internet will allow many informal and vocational courses more suitable for many illiterate or semi-literate population who dominate the base of the Pyramid people. Formal courses, whether for the beginners or for advanced students are not suitable for many people at the base of the pyramid as many have not attended schools—just might have learned how to read or write at home and yet many remained totally illiterate.

Accessing online books is another key factor that underdeveloped & developing countries can easily benefit from the Internet. In fact, new books (some may be audio only) can and should be written for illiterate population so that they can really learn and enjoy books on many topics.

To drive innovation and entrepreneurship, we would need to include relevant courses in the education system mentioned above. Such courses (both formal and informal) will inspire many students to focus on innovation and entrepreneurship. An important factor in this is to include "business school" and "business courses" for almost all students as this is critical for entrepreneurship and innovation. Many schools and universities do not have business school or have business school but it does not work closely with engineering, medical and science departments. This needs to be changed so that such institutions really teach materials that will help students to become innovators and entrepreneurs.

Another very important point in this regard is focusing on **multi-disciplinary education**. To be competitive and address local, regional and global needs, students today would need to learn not just one subject but multiple subjects. Thus, many universities, especially, in the developed world, have started offering multi-disciplinary degrees. A good example is **Stanford University** that started **Bio X dept.**—first marriage between engineering and medical school (X means multiple things including engineering, medical, pharmaceutical, informatics and more).

Besides, we would need to involve schools, colleges, universities, research institutes, computer training centers and many other institutions to actively promote innovation and entrepreneurship. In this regard, we would need to involve various organizations (including NGOs and Govts., and International bodies who care for global development). Thus, we would need to have some sort of well defined plan and system which would also need a good **business model** (as described in Chapter 9) to ensure that the whole ecosystem works well and sustainable for a long time with good growth.

Thus, good strategy, planning, implementation, continuous efforts, innovation and entrepreneurship for life with well coordination between various organizations using good business models are the keys—in other words continue to thrive, compete and prosper to do better and go to the top but with realistic goals and expectations. With such approach even if a country cannot reach to number one easily, can achieve number 2 or 3 or so with a very good economic growth. It does not always have to be within top 10 or so. As long as there are good prosperities from economic, social, cultural and other angles, it would be sufficient for many nations.

It is also important to note that despite our greatest efforts, some people may not learn well, may not be innovative well and may not be capable to do many things well. But that is o.k. as that is natural. There are needs for all types of people in this world—this is another type of pyramid (let's call it **workers pyramid**). Innovation/ creativity is also important in this pyramid. So we would need all types of hard working trained skilled people who can meet various needs.

In order to make innovation and entrepreneurship more focused and effective, a **"core competency"** would need to be developed. Not everyone can do everything. Similarly, not every country can do everything or should try to do everything. So, based on the capabilities, needs, growth plan, global needs and similar other factors, each country would need to define the areas it would need to focus so that it can surpass others in these areas, and thus get to a leadership position in such clearly defined areas. In general, since we are all part of globalization, we would need to keep in mind **the new technologies that will drive the world business for a long time. Five such technologies today are IT (information technology), Biotechnology, Nanotechnology, Alternate energy and their combination.** In order to develop good core competencies, **proper technologies would need to be transferred**, nurtured, used and well managed to develop new products/services that can be sold to local, regional and global markets.

Some Examples

It is important to show some examples to further clarify how education, innovation and entrepreneurship work together to drive developments. And, of course, Internet access is the key to have all these work together.

Emdad Khan

The economies of many underdeveloped and developing countries are based on agriculture. So, first I will give some examples to improve agriculture / farming related products and services in Zambia, Africa. This will be followed by some examples in India, U.S and some examples in organizations like UN. These are just a few selected examples. In general, both General Voice Internet and Custom Voice Internet are applicable for any country, and are used by many people worldwide.

Zambia [LinkUNICEF_Zambia], [LinkEISA_Zambia]

Country Scenario:

General—

1. 80% people below poverty level
2. Illiteracy rate—50% in the rural area, 33% in the urban area
3. only 1% of population are currently accessing the Internet.
4. 70% people are youth

Agriculture Related—

1. The cost of production is too high which makes produce in the country to be uncompetitive.
2. The cost of inputs is very high.
3. Low Productivity levels due to lack of extension services [refer to Appendix A for details], technology and funds going to wrong groups *[key groups e.g. "extension services" group are not getting appropriate amount of funding; rather other groups like supplier and support groups are getting good amount of funding]* resulting a very inefficient system (e.g. generating only 1 ton per Hector as opposed to expected 10 tons per Hector).
4. Problems of diseases in livestock.
5. The loss of animals also causes poverty as animals like cattle are wealth for farmers.
6. poor infrastructure such as roads.
7. The cost of borrowing is prohibitive. The interest rates are very high.

104

There is also no funds available for long term lending; limited funds are available only for short term and medium term .

8. Lack of technology and update of existing practices is difficult to get due to lack of extension services.

9. High waste of produce like tomatoes and mangoes because farmers don't have knowledge of how to preserve them and how to process them to convert into non-perishable items like convert tomatoes, mangoes in to tomato juice, mango juice; convert milk to cheese, butter, yogurt etc.

10. No simple outlets for farmers to sell easily.

Some Desired Solution:

a. Provide much improved extension services so that farmers become more knowledgeable in making their produce, processing their products, in getting supplies more easily, in selling their products more easily and the like; thus improving efficiency, increasing their margin and minimize loss of animals.

b. Make arrangement for long term funding as well as low interest rate based short term and medium term fundings.

c. Enable farmers to become innovative and entrepreneurial to further improve efficiency and also to come up with new products and services

d. Enable farmers to move up the food chain and become owners of food processing plants, food export process and the like

How Voice Internet Helps:

1. Provide basic farming related education to all farmers via any phone and user's voice (more on this with examples in Chapter 9).

2. Provide many Extension services via on-line using any phone.

3. Help farmers sell more easily via simple outlets.

4. Help farmers sell via online shopping portals.

5. Help farmers learn how to minimize waste and preserve their produce by converting them into various processed food products.

6. Help get funding through Voice Internet based Microfinance (more on this in Chapter 9)

All these help improve the efficiency significantly, make their selling process much easier, minimize waste and increase their ROI (Return on investment). Voice Internet based learning also enables them to move up the food chain and come up with new forms of products and services. Because most of them are illiterate and do not know how to read or write, Voice Internet is a very good affordable, easy to learn and easy to use practical way to help farmers. Once they become more efficient and improve their ROI, it will be easier for them to get more funding, especially long term loan (or some grants) so that they can expand their businesses in various ways and employ more people. E.g. some of the farmers would be able to learn enough to provide some key extension services face to face to those who may not be very comfortable to learn via phone (shyness, inertia to not learn anything new etc).

Above mentioned approaches with Voice Internet also work well for other applications including training in "village chicken commercial production" methods and use of its manure for bio gas energy production for lighting and cooking.

India

Family planning is very important in India to control population growth. The Government has started a program, very similar to IVR (Interactive Voice Response system), where people can call any time and ask questions about contraceptives to some live operators / teachers. These operators use on-line materials to quickly find the answers and convey that over the phone to the callers.

As the call volume increases, it becomes very **expensive to scale this up.** Here, Voice Internet becomes a nice efficient solution to provide the requested answers automatically to the callers. A small number of operators are kept to answer complex questions or for callers who would like to talk to a live agent.

Also, magnitude of the Digital Divide is high in India. The cell phone penetration is also very high resulting computer to cell phone ratio of less than 10%. Over 80% cell phones are basic cell phones and hence have SMS capability but no Internet capability. Thus, Voice Internet is a practical low cost solution for many people to enjoy the benefits of the Internet by accessing it as a general Internet Access service.

United States

The Digital Divide is relatively small in U.S except for some population like Native Indians and Alaskans. However, Digital Divide exists well for people with disabilities and also for elderly people. Thus, currently Voice Internet usage is dominated by blind and elderly people. It is important to note that that Voice Internet is good for such population in any country.

Voice Internet helps such users mainly to become more independent, getting jobs, doing existing jobs better, getting better entertainment, better rehabilitation, minimizing loneliness, improving social inclusion and stay connected.

The need to ensure that elderly people can continue to interact with the society, contribute to the society in various ways (especially with their wealth of experiences), and, of course contribute to their own lives is very well known. According to latest research, a person lives longer if he/she is challenged physically and mentally (i.e. physical exercise and exercise of the brain) and happy all the time. And if we can ensure all these, then a person not only will live longer happily but will also contribute to the society in a more effective way.

ICT based solutions to address above mentioned problems is critical, especially, because of the fact that we are in the Information Age and information & ICT are keys for social interaction, happiness, improving financial situation and more as evidenced by the Internet access and interacting with it (E.g. Facebook, U-tube, MySpace, . . .). Since it is difficult for people in this group to use conventional devices like a computer, PDA or high end cell phone, Voice Internet becomes a simple and affordable way to enjoy the key benefits of the Internet.

Entrepreneurship and Innovation are equally important for this population group—as we know people these days can easily live up to 100 years. With the current retirement age, many people do not have enough savings to live up to 100 year. In other words they would need some new sources of income. Thus, it is important that this population can learn about entrepreneurship and innovation so that they can start new businesses or work somewhere after gaining some new skills. One such key area is Health Care which is expensive and they would need to spend a major part of their savings for healthcare. By developing and using many Voice Internet based on-line healthcare services as appropriate, the overall healthcare expense can be minimized significantly.

United Nations

As mentioned in Chapter 1, UN took a new initiative to minimize poverty and improve the global distribution of wealth which is called the Millennium Development Goals (MDG). One of the key UN charter is to achieve the MDGs by 2015. Since base of the Pyramid people are the key in minimizing poverty (as they are the one below the poverty line), this population group must be involved in the process of poverty alleviation (and ultimately poverty eradication).

Poverty alleviation would not be possible without education, innovation and entrepreneurship. And, to make that happen, access to information is a must. Thus, Voice Internet is a key in providing Internet access (and hence access to all key information), and all the examples mentioned so far will directly or indirectly contribute to poverty eradication. Thus, more population from the base of the Pyramid would need to be included to access the information to truly achieve MDGs. In order to facilitate this UN GAID has created eMDG Portal to allow many people to share their thoughts on-line. This portal is also accessible by Voice Internet so that many users around the world can easily access the eMDG Portal by using voice & any telephone, and contribute in various ways to help achieve MDGs.

Chapter 9

Reshaping the Global Economy
by Bottom of the Pyramid People

"One should not pursue goals that are easily achieved. One must develop an instinct for what one can just barely achieve through one's greatest efforts"—Albert Einstein

In Chapter 8, I have shown why education, innovation and entrepreneurship are so important once the Digital and Language Divides are bridged from connectivity standpoint. A few examples are also provided to show how basic Internet access by Voice Internet along with the focus on education, innovation and entrepreneurship can help many people at the base of the pyramid in their economic, social, cultural and other developments.

However, to ensure that all these work in a sustainable way, the need for a business model was emphasized. In our efforts to reshaping the Global Economy by converting the base of the pyramid people into a valuable enormous resource by focusing on education, innovation and entrepreneurship, let me first describe the need for a **business model** in more details.

Ensure a good Model so that all Components Work in Harmony

As already mentioned, education needs to be reformed to focus on innovation, entrepreneurship as well as on immediate, short term and long term needs. But just teaching entrepreneurship and innovation is not going to suffice as these need to be actually practiced as well to make them really effective. So, we would need an environment to ensure that all these can work together in harmony. We would also need to make sure that such an environment can foster technology transfer, product and service development, business development, market capture, sustain and grow business, and these should be driven from a business stand point rather than good will, charity, ideas, or presenting papers in seminars and trade shows. Of course doing research, presenting papers, having discussion forums are very important key steps but to have a successful, effective, sustainable, growing system, it has to be driven and supported by a profitable business model. A successful profitable business model will provide incentives to

(a) technology providing entities to make the technology available,
(b) technology recipient companies to get the technology, localize it and refine it to sell in the local, regional and global markets,
(c) business providing entities to outsource the services and products,
(d) other participating entities in the food chain (e.g. companies or entities facilitating the technology transfer & outsourcing, research institutions, distributors, service providers, etc.).

Fig. 9.1 shows an example of a viable business model that shows all the key parties involved. An important key element in entrepreneurship and innovation driven business is to have nice working environment with investors, entrepreneurs, and skilled work forces. The proposed business model would ensure that such an environment exists. The model should also encourage universities and research institutions to work together to foster entrepreneurship and innovation by teaching both **business and technology together** (not as currently done in isolation in many universities in the underdeveloped and developing worlds) and help doing the related research.

With real contribution through knowledge power and cheaper labor managed by knowledge power, almost any country in the under developed and developing world can attract investors to invest, rather than get loan from the World Bank, IMF or other lending agencies with strong unfavorable terms. Yes, investors will also take good part of the profit but that's normal. If with investor's money other countries can flourish, so can many other developing & under developed countries. The goal should be to continue to move up the food chain by continuing innovation.

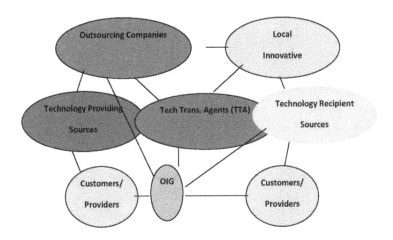

Fig. 9.1: An example of a viable Business Model. Customers / Providers are the companies getting the technology first and then get outsourced business from the outsourcing companies. Customers / Providers can also develop their own innovative products and services and sell in the local & global markets. TTA works as the main agent for the technology. OIG (Other Interested Groups) includes Investors, Government, NGOs, Foundations, Universities, Research Institutions and Partners.

Starting with Proven Business Models

Use of the proposed business model just mentioned is very important. But developing and refining such a business model may take some time. So, a more logical step would be to use some existing proven models while in parallel we focus on developing new business models. *Moreover, in some cases the already proven models can be significantly enhanced as shown in the two examples shown below.* I have used Voice Internet in these two examples, but the concept should apply to other technologies / businesses as well.

Microfinance Model with Higher ROI & Higher Participation

Before showing how Voice Internet fits with microfinance, let me explain the key idea that Voice Internet uses for fast global deployment. Voice Internet uses existing infrastructures and models when possible. E.g. it uses existing telephone network infrastructure. It uses people's existing phones and existing websites (without creating new sites by re-writing). And in the same way Voice Internet uses existing distribution channels like Service providers (e.g. telephone companies, wireless providers, Internet Service Providers—ISPs, Application Service Providers—ASPs).

In the same way, Voice Internet can successfully use existing microfinance infrastructure. In this case, however, Voice Internet can also help enhance the microfinance infrastructure and business model (this applicable for other infrastructures and business models as well). Let me explain this—the microfinance borrowers borrow a small amount of money and use it to do some business e.g. buy cows and sell milk. One of the main issues is that most borrowers do the same or similar things. Consequently, in a village, most borrowers are likely to sell milk to the same customers. This causes price competition resulting lower margin. In addition, the borrowers would need to return money back to lenders, usually every week, which puts extreme pressure on the borrowers (it is important to note that as a policy, Microfinance model does not provide any business idea, it just provides funding [Yunus2007]).

Now, let's say that in addition to lending money to the borrowers, we provide specific valuable information via the Internet (e.g. using Voice Internet) that can be used by the borrowers to do some innovative new businesses—e.g. a farmer can do better farming, sell produce with higher margin, learn how to preserve produces and minimize waste (refer to some key examples in Chapter 8) and many more. By providing such valuable information and associated training on entrepreneurship & innovation, many people will be able to come up with new compelling business ideas that can provide much higher financial & social **ROI *(Return on Investment) allowing them to keep more for themselves and also providing higher financial return to the lenders.***

***As reported in many texts, the interest rate for* microfinance is high** (can range from 30% to 60%). Higher ROI will alleviate this by a substantial amount. Use of the Internet and Voice Internet in processing microfinance would also reduce the management cost, thus lowering the high interest rate. Hence, Voice Internet enabled microfinance would attract many more lenders and borrowers in a positive win-win way—generating more revenues with higher ROI, lowering interest rate and also returning more to the lenders. Accordingly, it would make the microfinance model more successful and will strengthen the whole microfinance infrastructure. Apart from a higher financial ROI, there is obviously a strong Social ROI. And hence, it is a key driving force not just for traditional lenders, but also for many donors and companies to maintain their good corporate citizenship. **And, of course, it would also help Voice Internet significantly as many microfinance borrowers will use the Voice Internet service.**

This will also help the Social Business and Social Entrepreneurship. Yunus [Yunus2007] has defined two broad types of Social Businesses:

(1) Companies that focus on providing social benefits only rather than on maximizing profit.
(2) Profit-maximizing business (traditional mainstream businesses) but owned by the poor or disadvantaged.

It is the second type of Social Business that is more attractive and will be benefited more from the proposed model. This is because with the help of entrepreneurship & innovation, such businesses can solve some key problems at a lower cost and can come up with products and services that can be sold to the local, regional and global markets, resulting in **money to flow from rich to poor in a substantial amount**, which is very much needed for real global development. Without innovation & entrepreneurship, especially driven by IT, the Social Businesses will be focusing mainly the local market & local needs, and will be mainly addressing the need of poor people—thus, money will circulate mainly within the poor.

Voice Internet based microfinance process has already started in some African and Asian countries and we expect this to be followed in many other countries soon.

UN and MDG—Help Realizing MDGs with Voice Internet

As mentioned in Chapter 1 and Chapter 8, UN took a new initiative to minimize poverty and improve the global distribution of wealth which is called the Millennium Development Goals[2] (MDG). One of the key UN charter is to achieve the MDGs by 2015. Since base of the Pyramid people are the key in minimizing poverty (as they are the one below the poverty line), this population group must be involved in the process of poverty alleviation (and ultimately poverty eradication).

UN and its affiliate organizations have a strong drive in realizing MDG goals. Many governments are very actively involved in achieving MDGs. Many companies and organizations are also closely working with UN in this regard.

However, as already mentioned in Chapter 8, poverty alleviation would not be possible without education, innovation and entrepreneurship. And, to make that happen, access to information is a must. Thus, Voice Internet is a key in providing Internet access (and hence access to all key information), and all the examples mentioned so far will directly or indirectly contribute to poverty eradication. Hence, more population from the base of the Pyramid would need to be included to access the information to truly achieve MDGs. Accordingly, Voice Internet is mentioned through UN efforts as appropriate.

Also, in order to help achieve MDGs, UN GAID has created eMDG Portal to allow many people to share their thoughts on-line. This portal is also accessible by Voice Internet so that many users around the world can easily access the eMDG Portal by using voice & any telephone, and contribute in various ways to help achieve MDGs.

Resource Creation

In improving global economy and reducing rich-poor gap, we would need to focus on the fundamental components that drive economy. The four such major components are:

1. resources

2. education & knowledge
3. productivity
4. creativity & intelligence

Some of these are interdependent. For example, an educated person can create knowledge resource, a creative person can teach many people how to improve productivity, resources can help education and creativity. Such interdependencies need to be explored well. Some countries may have abundant natural resources but may not know (or may not have the drive to) how to use them and really grow the economy (a good example is oil rich countries). Resource can also be human resource to use their physical labor (like for manufacturing) or knowledge (like teaching or software development).

So, among all the 4 key components mentioned above, it is fair to say that the most important one is "education" as it can create other components. Once such components are created, job creation can easily follow and thus education drives the economy.

It is also fair to say that "creativity" is the second important factor as it can also develop other components. Once education can be used properly to develop some creativity, the economy can be improved in various ways and degrees.

Thus, education and creativity are the two very key components that can transform human resource into a great valuable resource that can help drive economy. Human resource of today's bottom of the pyramid will not be a social burden anymore rather a great contributing factor to the whole world. And by improving economy significantly will also drive social, cultural and other developments. Human resource is something that can be ported easily. Thus, having a god human resource, a country can export such resource to other countries where there are critical resource needs.

By "education", I do not necessarily mean just formal education and degrees. Education can be as simple as training some people to do some manufacturing job very well. For example, most workers in a garment industry do not have any formal education—they just know how to do their manufacturing job well (of course, some people with formal education are needed to manage, plan etc). So, the education needs to be creative and targeted to meet immediate needs. Creativity also depends on the need. If a country already has lot of skilled workers and doing well in improving economy, then the country's next goal is to keep on improving what it does better (to stay ahead of competition) and also innovate to diversify to move up the overall food chain of the economy.

Thus, education needs to be well planned as creativity is needed at various steps. The current education system in many underdeveloped and developing countries is "traditional" and mostly degree oriented. There needs to be a very good co-ordination between what a country's needs are and what educational institutions in the country produce. **To stimulate real economic growth, "education" needs to be targeted as mentioned, especially with "creativity", "productivity" and "resource" creation in mind. Creativity will in turn drive innovation, entrepreneurship, productivity (and even resources—like discovering new oil reserve, alternate energy . . .) resulting successful business entities which in turn will create jobs and drive economy.**

A few examples of innovation and entrepreneurship are provided in Chapter 8. As also explained, **Voice Internet is a key enabler of innovation and entrepreneurship**, especially for the bottom of the pyramid people. Thus, all the related examples provided so far are very closely related to **resource creation** and help driving economic, social, cultural and other developments. *A few examples of resource creation are also provided below.*

These examples show that education, innovation, creativity, productivity and resources are keys for initiating as well as sustaining economic growth. In general, the level of innovation / creativity has more influence to the level of the economic growth. So, innovation is very key for economic development. Without innovation we would be still hunting to meet our daily food needs.

It is important to note that innovation needs to be at all level; not just at high level like high tech. Converting base of the pyramid people into a huge resource would need many innovations, most of them would be at the basic innovation level. Thus, there is opportunity for everyone. And also there are needs for all types of people in the world. So we would need all types of hard working trained skilled people, based on their capability, desire to work hard and ambition.

To ensure an effective method for resource creation**, two fundamental** things needs to be realized by the rich and poor. The rich needs to realize that a huge resource can be developed in the poor people which can be very effectively used for global economic development with great financial returns to both the rich and the poor people. The poor would need to realize that their financial poorness is not a real shortcoming—it is just a temporary one and they can change their future by learning key things that can dramatically change their economic condition. Moreover, they can become a major global economic contributor. And government would need to realize the benefits as well. Besides, government would also need to facilitate as appropriate so that the rich can work more effectively with the poor, and the poor can get initial boost needed before blessed by rich.

In summary,

(a) Bridge the **Digital Divide and Language Divide** in a practical and effective way.
(b) Use the benefits of bridging the Digital & Language Divides to provide useful, targeted and **valuable education**.
(c) Focus on sustainable growth (economic, social, cultural, . . .) by **creating a huge resource** through **education, innovation and entrepreneurship**.
(d) Ensure a good model to tie (a), (b) and (c).

Examples of Resource Creation
(using Education, Innovation and Entrepreneurship)

As already mentioned, all the examples provided so far are very closely related to **resource creation** and help driving economic, social, cultural and other developments. Here, we provide a few examples of **resource creation** and discuss all related issues at a more detailed level so that all key parties involved (including the entrepreneurs and innovators) are very clear about the process, their roles and how resources can be created successfully.

In Fig. 9.1 we have shown two circles, namely, "Local Innovative Products & Services" and "Customers / Providers". Key driving forces for these groups (especially the group driving Local Innovative Products & Services) are the entrepreneurs and innovators. They will come up with new ideas mainly to solve their problems using the technologies that are affordable and easily available. In many cases such technologies would be available locally. In some cases such technologies would need to be transferred from some developed countries using the TTA (Technology Transfer Agents as shown in Fig. 9.1) or directly from the technology providers. Other groups would need to be involved to implement their ideas (using a Business Plan as appropriate)—such groups include funding institutions (including MF, NGOs, Govts, Venture Capitals), TTAs, research institutions and others as shown in Fig. 9.1. What we focus here is more details of innovation and entrepreneurship done by the bottom of the pyramid people driven by education. There are three broad scenarios:

a. Educated / semi educated people who have the potential to learn relatively higher level skills in some high impact focus areas including ICT, farming and manufacturing.
b. Semi-literate or illiterate people who can learn some lower and medium level skills.
c. Illiterate people who can learn some basic and lower level skills.

In all these three cases, there will be a good percentage of people who would be able to use their skills to come up with new ideas to do businesses with new products and services. These cases are discussed below in more details. The "illiterate" case is described first as illiterate people are at the bottom of the pyramid.

Illiterate People

Extension services was briefly introduced in Chapter 8 [refer to Appendix A for details]. Such extension services basically provide important information about various topics (e.g. farming) to the base of the pyramid people. Instructors usually go to rural areas and teach / inform farmers about the latest technologies, methods and the like so that farmers can improve their efficiency, increase food production, increase their revenue and ROI (Return on Investment). However, such extension services are scarce in the underdeveloped and developing countries—e.g.in Zambia, Africa. Voice Internet provides all such key information from a nice "farming portal" over any phone; thus making voice based on-line Extension Services, and helping many people at the base of the pyramid to improve their economy. To further clarify, I use "How to Preserve Mangoes" as an example as many mangoes get wasted on a regular basis. Of course, the same concept applies for many other fruits, vegetables, meat, fish and more. It also applies for many non-farming applications.

The following three examples are taken from Google Search on "How to Preserve Mangoes?" (the concept would work even in a better way when the information is taken from a "Farming portal").

[NOTE: Author is not responsible for the accuracy / validity of the the following information in #a, #b and #c]

Preserving mangoes for at least two months (From Google Search)

    a.   Yahoo [LinkMangoPreserve1]
          PRESERVE MANGOES? YES, YOU CAN!

Want to preserve some tasty mangoes for another day?

The tropical fruit can be canned or frozen for use later, according to the U.S. National Center for Home Food Preservation.

Here is how:

- Selection: According to Pete Luckett, forget what you've learned about other fruit as "a good mango may be as hard as a turnip or as soft as a ripe avocado. The leathery skin may be thick or thin, smooth and taut or gently wrinkled."

  Smell the stem end and avoid those that give off a kerosene aroma as they might be overripe. Choose those that smell sweet.

- Ripening: Under ripe mangoes can be ripened at home out of the fridge and away from direct sunlight.

- Cutting: Hold the mango toward you on its narrow side, and slice down on one side of the seed. Then make a similar cut on the other side. With the two seedless pieces, you can peel them and slice as you like. Or, by holding the mango skin side down, use a knife to score the fruit without going through the skin. Then fold the skin inside out and slice from the skin or serve as is.
- Freezing: Wash, peel and slice. Arrange slices on a flat pan and freeze. Once frozen, store in a plastic freezer bag or sealed containers. Or puree slices in a blender or food processor. Sugar can be added if preferred and then pack into containers and freeze.
- Canning: Pack slices into jars. Cover with a 30% syrup solution. (To ensure proper food safety, use a canning guide).

b. Yahoo [LinkMangoPreserve2]

1. Remove tops of mangoes. Remove peels with your hands. Do not use peeler. With a knife cut slices as thick or thin as you like. Thicker slices taste better.
2. When all possible slices have been removed, extract juice from the mango. In a broad-bottomed vessel place the mango slices and juice and cover with sugar. One and half kg sugar to 1 kg mango slices. Keep aside for some time
3. Stir the sugar. Keep on high flame till it boils. Lower flame. Let it boil till golden yellow and thick.
4. Add 1tsp citric acid to 1 kg mangoes or till it is sour enough to suit your taste
5. Add half tsp meta-bi-sulphite after mixing with a little syrup and stir well. Cool and fill in bottles.

c. IndianExpress [LinkMangoPreserve3]

Pune (India)—Based entrepreneur Rajiv Devkar seems to have hit the jackpot in his quest to preserve mangoes without the use of cold storage facilities. Devkar experimented with honey, a natural preservative as an alternative, putting two alphonso mangoes in a jar of honey in May and found them well-preserved in December. Armed with some lab results and investment partners, he decided to expand the scope of his experiment.

"I wanted to preserve mangoes without using anything artificial and it occurred to me that honey has been used as a preservative since ancient times," said Devkar, explaining what he sees as a 'win-win' scenario. "Indians love mangoes. They would definitely pay a substantial amount—to eat the fruit through out the year. On the other hand, mango growers would get a much better margin for their crops in the off season," he said.

To obtain scientific backing for his claim Devkar got the mango samples tested with the first lab report coming through three months ago. "The mango looked edible. It was in its natural state and natural colour, although the sugar content was slightly higher because it was dipped in honey," said R S Waghmare, Deputy Director of the State Public Health Laboratory and Director of Pune Food Laboratory.

As you can see, using Voice Internet based extension service, any illiterate person from the bottom of the pyramid can easily access such information, learn the process and use it in his / her daily life. **As we know, in this Information Age, information is money like "Time is Money". This is a great example of how to successfully use very relevant information by an illiterate person.** This can also be achieved even without Extension Services; and rather just using Voice Internet service and using the Search Feature of the Voice Internet.

As already mentioned, some people from this group will also come up with new business ideas using the new information from which they have been deprived till now.

Semi-Literate and Semi-Educated group

People under this groups can use the benefits / capabilities of the newly created resource (e.g. a good number of people who learned how to preserve mangoes well) to come up with new business ideas. For example, some people will start making nice, easy to use and valuable "information portals" including "How to Preserve Mangoes?" Portal. Similarly, they can create and provide various Voice Internet based e-Learning courses more suitable for the base of the pyramid people. The same applies for e-Health, e-Gov and many other e-Services. Thus, semi-literate people will learn a lot about new things and how to use such information to create more resources from the base of the pyramid and also make them as a new source for the "Educated people" as described below. Such semi-literate and semi-educated people will be mainly creating their market by selling their products and service to the newly created "resource" from the illiterate people.

Educated People:

Educated people can go one step further by creating more complex applications. For example, they can create various applications for on-line transactions so that the illiterate and semi-literate people can easily sell to the buyers, bypassing many middlemen and increasing their ROI.

Educated people can do many more businesses as well by using their newly created resources and sell various new products & services to the local, regional and also global markets. For example, once a good number of educated people will successfully learn how to do various complex on-line transaction based applications, their resource can be used by medium and big companies for outsourcing as such newly created resource from the underdeveloped and developing countries would be much cheaper. Another example is to learn many other things (from both breadth and depth standpoints) so that they can become

a. a greater and much broader Outsourcing Resource
b. innovators & entrepreneurs developing new products and services good for the regional and global markets.

As mentioned in Chapters 7 & 8, **multi-disciplinary education** is very important to be competitive in this global world, especially to help innovation, entrepreneurship and solve many complex problems. To be competitive and address local, regional and global needs, students today would need to learn not just one subject but multiple subjects. Thus, many universities, especially, in the developed world, has started offering multi-disciplinary degrees. A good example is **Stanford University** that started **Bio X dept.**—first marriage between engineering and medical school (X means multiple things including engineering, medical, pharmaceutical, informatics and more).

The course curricula designed for institutions in developed countries are, in general, not suitable for the underdeveloped and developing countries. The problems and the needs of the bottom of the pyramid are different. Thus, directly using course curricula from the developed countries may produce graduates not suitable to get jobs in the local market. They are sort of more prepared for the developed country but going to another country and working there have other issues, and not so easy. Besides, even though they are more prepared for the developed countries, they are also not so well educated for the developed countries as they usually do not get a good education for many courses (designed for the developed world) due to lack of good instructors, laboratories, relevant industries and the like. So, such graduates usually would need to go to some developed countries to do further studies. Universities of the developed countries also encourage such students to join them as such institutions get many good students from around the world. However, many of them either do not get admitted or cannot afford to study abroad. Some graduates who get admitted, can afford and complete their study successfully usually get jobs abroad and do not go back to their home countries. This, although seems to be bad, is good in general as such graduates do well in abroad, remit a good amount of money to their home countries and help in many other ways including technology transfer, outsourcing, consulting and the like.

But since most of the graduates stay at home, let's focus on them. If courses can be designed so that they are more appropriate for the underdeveloped and developing countries in solving their immediate, short-term and long-term problems, then such graduates could contribute a lot in creating very appropriate resources very much needed for their countries. Note that in such a design process, knowledge from the good courses in the developed countries should be used as appropriate, and need to be matched and modified to fit with the local needs. This is also true for informal courses. Once this step is done successfully, then courses designed mainly for the developed world would gradually become more appropriate for the underdeveloped and developing world. Moreover, by creating a great resource and thus learning how to do the outsourcing well, learning how to develop new products and services and selling them locally, regionally and to some extend globally, such a resource will be ready to learn more and use the course curricula of the developed countries more effectively.

Moreover, at that point, they will design high level course curricula and also write books that some developed countries would be able to use, resulting in a more effective collaboration between the underdeveloped, developing and the developed countries.

As already mentioned, creation of such an enormous valuable resource is only possible by properly involving

    A. all key players, namely.
        1. illiterate, semi-literate & literate people.
        2. Universities, research institutions and similar institutions.
        3. Govts., NGOs and other organizations.
        4. Technology Transfer Agents.
        5. Businesses.
        6. Funding institutions.
        7. And all others as appropriate.

And
    B. By using a good Business Model (Fig. 9.1).

And creation of such an enormous resource will in turn result economic and various other developments (as described below) in a sustainable way with very good growth.

How Resource Creation Will Help Global Economy?

As explained in the previous Section, bridging the **Digital Divide and Language Divides,** using the benefits of bridging the Digital & Language Divides to provide useful, targeted and **valuable education,** focusing on sustainable growth by **creating a huge valuable resource** through **education, innovation and entrepreneurship,** and ensuring a good model to tie all these will result economic, social, cultural and other developments. But how exactly? In this Section, I explain this with special emphasis on **Economic development** as that in turn will help social, cultural and other developments. To explain it better, a brief review of existing economic situation and how we got here is described first using some key comments from some experts.

A Brief Review of Today's Economic System, How we Got Here and Looking Ahead

As mentioned in Chapter 1, in this world of over 6.5 billion people, over 4 billion people are poor—40% live in poverty, and 16% live in extreme poverty. The World Bank defines poverty as living on less than $2 a day, absolute or extreme poverty as living on less than $1 a day. Nobel Laureate Joseph Stiglitz in his fascinating latest book "Making Globalization Work[1]" says "Think for a minute what it means to live on one or two dollars a day. Life for people this poor is brutal. Childhood malnutrition is endemic, life expectancy is often below fifty years, and medical care is scarce. Hours are spent each day searching for fuel and drinkable water and . . . .". Apart from inadequate income, two other issues are heavily associated with people living below the poverty line: insecurity and powerlessness. One World Bank report published a nice statement from a young poor woman in Jamaica that captures the sense of powerlessness: "Poverty is like living in jail, living under bondage, waiting to be free". In general, poor have few opportunities to speak out. When they speak, no one listens; when someone does listen, the reply is that nothing can be done; when they are told something can be done, nothing is ever done.

Gap Between the Rich and Poor

The world is in a race between economic growth and population growth. So far the population growth is winning. Although the percentage of people living in poverty is falling, the absolute number is rising. About 25,000 people die every day of hunger or hunger-related causes, according to the United Nations. This is one person every three and a half seconds. Unfortunately, it is children who die most often.

The following two paragraphs from "The Economics on Trial" by Mark Skousen [Skousen1991] are worth noting:

*"**Yet there is plenty of food in the world for everyone.** The problem is that hungry people are trapped in severe poverty. They lack the money to buy enough food to nourish themselves. Being constantly malnourished, they become weaker and often sick. This makes them increasingly less able to work,*

which then makes them even poorer and hungrier. This downward spiral often continues until death for them and their families.

We all want to have a comfortable amount of money even with a little extra for treats now and then. Some people don't have a penny. Some people have millions and billions of dollars. The rich, if they give any to the poor give a small amount. People who are comfortable or people who are struggling find money for the needy. If you are rich instead of buying $50 to $100 jeans, give the money to the poor, buy them clothes, or give them your used clothes. Money isn't everything, though. The rich are greedy and the poor are needy. When will it stop? When will the greed for money die? Will it ever die?"

Now, let us take a look at economic situation from the past to present (from year 500), as shown in Fig. 9.2 below.

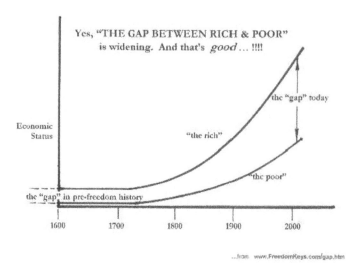

Yes, "THE GAP BETWEEN RICH & POOR" is widening. And that's *good* ... !!!!

the "gap" today

Economic Status

"the rich"

"the poor"

the "gap" in pre-freedom history

1600   1700   1800   1900   2000

...from www.FreedomKeys.com/gap.htm

Fig. 9.2 Rich-poor gap from the past until today. Courtesy: Economics on Trial—THE FREEMAN

One Graph Says It All—By Mark Skousen

Clearly, the rich poor gap is increasing as Fig. 9.3 shows. Economic growth was non-existent during the centuries 500-1500, and per capita GDP rose by merely 0.1 percent per year in the centuries 1500-1700.

The rich poor gap was very small as there was no real economic growth. As we entered into the agriculture revolution, followed by industrial revolution, the rich-poor gap started increasing sharply. This is strongly correlated with the economic growth. For example, Europe grew as high as 300% during this period (the re-building of Europe after World War II is a significant contributor to this high growth). The economic growth continued to increase as we entered into the Information Age, and so is the rich-poor gap. However, by moving from the old **"The big-government economy"** to the recent **"free market economy",** the situation shows to improve significantly as shown in Fig. 9.3 [Skousen1991]. In other words, the gap between the rich and poor in Fig.9.2 would be larger around year 2000 if major countries in the world had stayed with "big-government economy" model.

But the trend is clear i.e. the rich-poor gap is increasing at a high rate and it will continue as we enter into "Knowledge Economy" and then to "Intelligence Economy" unless we do something different fundamentally.

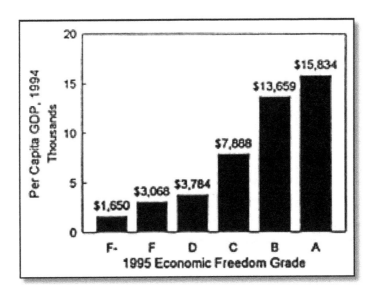

Fig. 9.3: Per Capita GDP versus Economic Freedom Grade. If ever a picture was worth a thousand words, this graph is it. Courtesy—Prof. James Gwartney et al, Florida State University.

Emdad Khan

World Economic System

Now, let's take a high level view of the world economic system. To get started, I use some facts ([Piasecki2007], [Yunus2007]):

1. 51 of the 100 largest economies in the world are now corporations, not nations.
2. They are massive mentions unto themselves who have great political leverage.
3. The 100 largest multinational corporations (MNCs) now control about 20% of global foreign assets. These top 100 are household names.
4. 300 MNCs-conglomerates such as Honeywell, IBM, DuPont, DOW and Whirlpool—now account for 25%of the Worlds total assets, a sizeable impact.
5. As much as 40% of world trade now occurs within these top multinationals, which explains why they are studied and emulated by smaller companies.
6. Only 21 nations have gross domestic product markets larger than the annual sales revenue of each of the 6th largest multinational corporations.
7. In 2000, richest 1% owned 40% of world's asset and richest 10% owned 85% of world's asset. In contrast, the bottom half of the world population owned barely 1% of the world's asset.
8. China, India and Indonesia have 42% of the world's population but receive only 9% of world's income.
9. 50 million richest people in the world (the top 1 %) receive as much income as the bottom 57% (over 3 billion people).

Thus, the size and global scope of a few companies, governments and individuals control our world. This is the key reason for the widening gap between the rich and poor. *This does not seem to be done intentionally, rather this is a trap (a key feature of the capitalism) we have fallen into—rich get richer and poor get poorer (further explained below).*

Now let's take a look at the money flow i.e. funding / debt system.

128

In the old days many countries used Gold as the reserve. But as some currency, especially, dollar became very stable and strong, most of the countries today buy US Treasury bills (T-Bill) or dollars as their reserve. It is very important to have a good level of reserve to get loans from rich countries or international organizations like the IMF (International Monetary Fund) and the World Bank. Developing countries need loans as they do not have enough funding of their own to accomplish their planned development efforts.

As nicely stated by Nobel Laureate Joseph Siglitz [Siglitz2006], "The richest country in the world, the United States, seemingly cannot live within its means, borrowing $2 billion a day from poorer countries". What it means is that poorer countries are buying US T-bills and that to its reserve. More importantly, the level of reserve is increasing with a good rate. In just four years between 2001 and 2005, eight East Asian countries (Japan, China, South Korea, Singapore, Malaysia, Thailand, Indonesia and the Philippines) more than doubled their total reserves from roughly $1 trillion to $2.3 trillion. "By the end of 2006, developing country reserves are estimated to reach $3.35 trillion" [Stiglitz2006].

These dollars are mainly re-invested (by lending) to the developing countries with about 20% interest rate. The interest paid to the T-Bill holders is under 5% in general. Thus, a net of about 15% interest flows every year to the United States from the developing countries which amounted to about $600 billion in 2006. This is obviously a great deal for U.S but a bad deal for the developing countries. What would have happened if US did not lend this money? Well, if so, two major things would have happened

(a) developing countries would be in financial trouble without any real development. In other words even though the cost to the money they borrowed is very high, they still get a good return if they use the money wisely. Some corrupt countries use only a small part of the money for development and hence the net development may be very insignificant.

(b) Without a very stable currency (like US dollar or Euro), the fear of weak global economy might start causing prices to fall causing deflation that plagued Japan for a decade.

So, the question really is, "is there a way to improve this so that developing countries would not have to pay such a high cost?" This is a big question that many people, organizations, universities, research institutions and the like have been asking.

Can Current Model Really Bridge the Rich-Poor Gap?

Clearly, current approaches are better than the approaches used before in improving the economy worldwide. From Fig. 9.2, we see that both top and bottom curves are moving up. This means that economy is improving for both rich and poor. So, the free market economy model is great and should be continued.

However, the gap is also increasing as already mentioned—this is why many people say, the rich are getting richer and poor are getting poorer. The goal is to minimize this gap. Obviously, this gap will not be minimized by just continuing with current approaches as the trend is to increase the gap using current approaches rather than decreasing.

The cause of this increasing gap is supported by the above mentioned fact that few large companies, governments and individuals control our world. Continuing the same way will just strengthen the control of these companies, governments and individuals. In fact, it even will further increase the power of such companies, and more and more governments will be controlled by such corporation as they will control more of the financial system.

Strong influence of such very large corporations in a way inhibits formation of new entrepreneurial and innovative companies from the base of the pyramid people as entrepreneurs fear that whatever idea / products they come up with will be possibly done by the big companies, or their ideas will be taken away when they approach such companies for investment fund, or once they develop some products, such big companies will do similar products and sell at a much lower cost to drive such entrepreneurs away. Only a few entrepreneurs get lucky when they come up with such a new idea that large companies cannot do that well or cannot do that quickly and finally buy such small companies. While this type of fear is truc for some cases, the entrepreneurs at the base of the pyramid also get incentives and encouragements to do something new from the examples set by some recently formed large corporations e.g. Google, Facebook and Twitter.

As mentioned in Chapter 1, further increase of the power of such large companies, and that more and more governments will be controlled by such corporation as they will control more of the financial system is also reflected by comments from high level experts. Some comments & recommendations made by Nobel Laureate Stiglitz to improve the situation are repeated below for convenience [Stiglitz2006]:

"In spite of so much works done by so many organizations (including the World Bank and IMF—International Monetary Fund), the poverty has been increasing rather than decreasing. Key reasons for so are:

(a) Organizations (including corporations) involved in this process try to solve it but without really giving up their key goals like high profitability and having good financial control. Associated policies actually helped lenders much more and borrowers much less.

(b) Because of (a), many governments took loan with unfavorable terms and paying high interest; thus forcing them to spend less on the development. It has caused a big "debt burden" for many countries. It has also contributed to the global financial instability.

(c) The need for "reserve" for each country (indirectly came from the Global financial system), caused money to actually flow from poor to the rich (instead of the other way around)—for example US is borrowing (or developing and poor countries are lending) $2B per day (this figure is lowered to some extent after the financial melt-down during end of 2008) by selling its T-Bill with a very low interest rate. If this money could be lent at higher interest rate or not lend at all, each country could spent the same for key development. This has resulted an unstable Global Reserve system.

(d) Economic globalization has outpaced political globalization.

(e) Globalization without good Global rule."

NOTE: In above, Stiglitz is saying "the poverty has been increasing rather than decreasing". This is even worse as Fig. 9.2 shows poverty is decreasing but the rich-poor gap is increasing.

Stiglitz has also made comments about U.N efforts in this regard:

"The UN's effort to combat poverty with an organized institutional plan is something that is greatly needed. Private giving, through individuals or small groups, is not enough to bring the poverty level down as much as we would like. This system of private giving is too disorganized to be effective. The UN's plan is designed to combine funds from small contributors along with national contributions in order to receive the money that is needed. This is a great method because individuals can be sure that they are helping to fund a project that is backed by the countries of the United Nations. This is an incentive to give because the United Nations is reputable and respected, and those who help to fund the project will know that their money is in good hands."

Stiglitz recommendations include

1. A new World Financial Reserve System that help money flow from rich to poor.
2. Democratization of Globalization.
3. Strengthening political globalization to be comparable with economic globalization.
4. Making the trade fair between rich and poor countries.
5. A good and stable way to eliminate the burden of debt.
6. Improving corporate role for social responsibility, less cost for poor countries, less profit from poor countries, limiting the power of corporations, improving corporate governance, and reducing the scope of corruption."

Such suggested policies, recommendations and plans are very good. However, as Stiglitz pointed out (as mentioned in Chapter 1), implementation of these proposed solutions would be difficult mainly because the stake holders would not really giving up their key goals like high profitability and having good financial control whereas the suggested recommendations do not encourage high profitability and high financial control for valid reasons.

A Proposed Model to Minimize the Rich-Poor Gap More Effectively

As mentioned in Chapter 1, the recommendations made in this book are mainly to bridge the Digital Divide which in turn will help reduce the rich-poor gap and other gaps. So, I am not trying to provide very specific solutions to minimize the rich-poor gap. However, the recommendations made below are mainly based on general concept and analysis, and would help minimize the rich-poor gap.

The approaches mentioned by Stiglitz and others are undoubtedly very good approaches and should be implemented when possible. However, most of these are at very high level. To really minimize all gaps, especially, rich-poor gap, we would need more specifics, especially complementary recommendations at implementation level so that we can achieve the desired goals. In fact, for some of the key problems, we would need to look at from **bottom-up standpoint**. A good example is converting the base of the pyramid people (mainly poor people) into a **huge valuable resource rather than keeping them as a social burden (one key topic of this Chapter)** by involving them as part of the solution rather than as part of the problem.

It is important to note that recommendations mentioned by many experts are to mainly improve global financial and economic planning. However, we would also need to keep in mind the following facts:

1) no matter how we look at it, the world is controlled by big corporations and rich people including big governments. So, whatever policies are made to ease the situation will still be made mainly to protect the interests of this rich population.

2) These big forces would also like to make sure that the rest of the world becomes a better world as if the neighbor is good, it is easier to live with etc. This is a positive sign but not at the cost of #1.

3) With better policies, plan, budget etc, the developing and underdeveloped countries still may not be able to avail the benefits

(e.g. investors would move to other countries if prices are raised etc) i.e. the governments may not have much power.

So, even though better policies are very important, to really help base of the pyramid people, we would need to look at it from bottom-up standpoint rather than top-down policy making and corresponding implementation standpoint.

The recommendations made by Paul Polak, C.K Prahlad, and many others (Chapter 1) at a medium and bottom levels are also very good recommendations to get out of poverty, and should be continued and enhanced when possible. But to do even better, especially, for the extremely poor (to not just get out of poverty but be financially more successful), we would need to do more.

The **recommendations made in this chapter and in this book are applicable for extremely poor, poor, middle class and to some extent for rich people.** By "truly" **Bridging the Digital Divide**, we can enable such people to focus on education; and by going beyond bridging the Digital Divide, these people can focus **on entrepreneurship and innovation** resulting real economic, social and other developments for themselves, and a huge low cost resource for rest of the world. This will also indirectly help some of the issues mentioned by Stiglitz.

For example, it will help global reserve system (repeated from Chapter 1 for convenience). Why? Well, if we analyze carefully, the real reason, countries are buying T-Bills mainly from US, in spite of such a high cost, is to ensure that their economy is less volatile—providing higher confidence to others to do business and trade with them. But then why mainly US T-Bill? Because as a country and its currency, US is very stable that one can really depend on (this is changing to some extent because of the recent financial melt-down but many still believe that US will come out of such down-turn soon). And the real reason for US stability is because of its **much sustained innovation and entrepreneurship for a long time.** *The same can be true (at least to a good extent) if a poor or developing country can really start doing innovation and entrepreneurship, and make & sell new products/services globally. When this happens, the need to keep high "reserve"* *will be minimized and other countries will have much more confidence on any country really creating and selling new products and services worldwide.*

Truly bridging the Digital Divide will also extend some of the ideas that Paul, Prahlad and others have mentioned. For example, helping the people in slums with the benefits of the Internet, entrepreneurship and innovation will enable them to do much more in increasing their income and society's income.

It is also important to show a few more examples how creating a huge resource by converting base of the pyramid people can help global economy. In fact such a proposed huge resource will start contributing in a major way to the world economy.

Once a low cost huge skilled resource is available to rich people, they will realize that it would be much better to work with such new emerging intelligent population, rather than try to ignore their efforts. This will result significant outsourcing of tasks to such population (see below for more).

Thus, **money will automatically start flowing from rich to the poor.** Today, money flows mainly within rich and some semi-rich (or mid level) skilled people; almost no money flows to the base of the pyramid people as they have no skills to help rich people in any way except some cheap manual labor.

Various relatively new methods (e.g. Social Businesses) mainly help circulate money within the poor. These are great methods and should be continued and expanded without any doubt. But to minimize the rich-poor gap and for poor to become part of the main stream economic system, money has to flow from rich to poor in a substantial way; and that is possible via valuable resource creation from the bottom of the pyramid people. We have already seen two such great successful examples—**China and India**.

Bottom of the pyramid skilled people will also start their own businesses, develop products and services that will help their needs more, and thus save money as currently they would need to buy all key technologies, products and services from companies dominated or owned by rich people at higher price. ***Such entrepreneurs will develop products and services mainly addressing their needs i.e. will focus on "design for bottom 90%" philosophy.*** Another key philosophy such entrepreneurs can and should follow is ***"Put Intelligence in Products & Services".*** Here "intelligence" mean intelligent User Interface, intelligent computation, intelligent processing and intelligent delivery. ***This will help such entrepreneurs (and hence the base of the pyramid people) to leapfrog*** in many areas.

Such entrepreneurs are encouraged to get initial funding from various sources other than very large corporations to protect their (such SMB's) interest (refer to the Section with title "Can Current Model Really Bridge the Rich-Poor Gap?" above) unless they are sure that they can protect their interests when working with large corporations.

Bottom of the pyramid people will be able to create competitive new products and services that can be sold to rich people at much lower price (e.g. the products and services developed with the philosophy of ***"design for bottom 90%"*** would also be attractive to many rich people). This will also help significant amount of **money to flow from the rich to the poor**. Fig. 9.4 shows all keys ways money can flow from rich to poor in a natural way and thus can help minimize the rich-poor gap significantly.

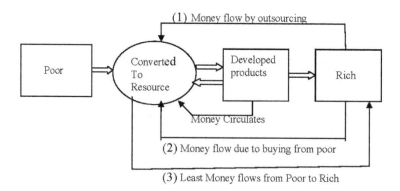

Fig. 9.4: Keys ways money can flow from rich to poor in a natural way and thus help minimize the rich-poor gap significantly. Note on (3): Least Money Flows from Poor to Rich as poor will only buy high end items that they would not be able to make.

Once a few small and medium companies from the bottom of the pyramid people will start doing successful business and show the world that more money started flowing from the rich to the poor using the approaches just mentioned, the number of such small and medium companies (SMBs) will grow fast, resulting in a steep growth. Thus, there will be millions of smaller size corporations (as opposed to a few large one) driving / reshaping world economy. This model is already validated today—e.g. in U.S., SMBs drive the economy. By using the proposed converted huge resource, SMBs will help drive the whole world economy. And there will also be some very large corporations from these new SMBs. Thus, apart from SMBs, there will be more balanced large corporations—from the rich world as well as from the poor world.

A few successful outsourcing models are worth mentioning—

Countries moving up the food chain in manufacturing (like China) has to outsource lower level tasks to other countries, like Vietnam. Many other countries can copy this process without too much efforts. Similarly, India is trying to move up the food chain in software and service related businesses. Many developing countries can do the same. China and India are two good examples that played the game in the right way and hence in fact became a friend of the countries controlling the world. The same is also true for Japan, Israel. It is started to happen in Russia, Brazil and some east European countries.

With real contribution through knowledge power and cheaper labor managed by knowledge power, almost any 3rd world countries can attract investors to invest, rather than get loan from the World Bank or IMF with strong unfavorable terms. Yes, investors will also take good part of the profit but that's normal. If with investor's money other countries can flourish, so can many other developing countries. The goal should be to continue to move up the food chain by continuing innovation. With investment from such investors, SMBs in the underdeveloped and developing world will be able to better monetize their proposed huge resource in an accelerated way; thus greatly contributing to their own economy as well as to the world economy (as large corporations will be able to produce their products at a lower price resulting higher sales and higher margins).

The Power of IT

IT is, in fact, a real mover and shaker. This is a technology that bottom of the pyramid people can use to jump forward fast. We have seen how many illiterate rural people were able to learn and use cell phones, many of whom never seen or use a landline phone. Voice Internet takes this power of IT to the bottom of the pyramid people in a meaningful, easy to use & learn, and a very cost effective way. Thus Voice Internet and associated technologies can transform the **Digital Divide to Digital Opportunity** fast worldwide. In fact, the adoption of Voice Internet and associated technologies show strong promise to develop "Digital Aladdin's Lamp" (a simple device that would provide answers to most common questions asked verbally) that Yunus [Yunus2007] has envisioned.

How Resource Creation will also Help Social, Cultural, other Developments & World Peace?

Apart from helping the economic development and help minimizing rich-poor gap, the proposed "resource creation" will also help in other various ways including social, cultural, political & other developments as well has help increase world peace.

Social Development

Social development is a very broad term and this is not a book to cover the details of social development. Sometimes it is also combined with socio-economic development. The idea here is to summarize how economic development fueled by information access, education, entrepreneurship and innovation can help improve the society in a significant way. For example, economic development will enable many people not to starve, have better food, better health, enable the country develop better infrastructure and the like. Thus, the society, in general will advance resulting less aggression, less violence, less terrorism, and the like which in turn will result a happier society.

A happier society would allow people to become more educated, more knowledgeable, more capable etc. This would help the society to move from, say feudalism to capitalism to something that I would like to call **"knowledge-ism"**. What is knowledge-ism?

Well, before defining it, let us see where we are headed. The societies in many countries moved from feudalism to capitalism during last few hundred years.

Capitalism brought lots of good things and, thus, although subjective, many people believe it is better than feudalism and communism / socialism. However, capitalism has negatives as well. One key negative is that capitalism help rich to get richer and poor to get poorer. As described, by creating a huge resource from the base of the pyramid people will enable money and wealth to flow from rich to poor naturally, and will help this world to be more balanced. In addition to money, base of the pyramid people will acquire valuable knowledge and the world will be a "knowledge driven society" where the value is "knowledge" rather than traditional "capital" which usually means money, land and other materials. So, I would like to call it **"knowledge-ism"**. This has several advantages and eliminates the key problems of capitalism—first, acquisition of knowledge (compared to acquisition of money) would be easier by all, especially poor people; second, knowledge would help better understand the humanity, not to be too greedy for money, and thus would help drive social ROI—rather than Financial ROI; and third, knowledge at the base of the pyramid people would drive more money to flow from rich to poor as rich will have a low cost good resource. Thus, **knowledge-ism would eliminate all major negatives of capitalism and would significantly help improve the societies around the world.**

What would be after "knowledge-ism"? Possibly, "intelligent-ism" as intelligence will drive all major things.

Cultural Development

Cultural development is often combined with socio-cultural evolution and associated development. This is not a book to cover the details of socio-cultural and cultural development. The idea here is to summarize how economic & social developments fueled by information access, education, entrepreneurship and innovation can help the cultural development. The key point to note in this regard is the multi-cultural aspect and cultural fusion. With access to the information (which expedited the globalization), societies can see the various cultures from other societies and there is a common trend to borrow more stuff from other culture resulting enhanced culture as well as cultural fusion. This is not just limited to what is meant by "cultural development" in a traditional way but also bringing new things to this. For example, cultural development may now mean to learn more and increase knowledge in history, evolution and other key areas. It may mean for a country to become more entrepreneurial by making "entrepreneurship" in citizens culture. And thus, cultural development is strongly influenced and changed by the ability to access to the information.

Political Development

Political development is very important and critical, especially in the underdeveloped and developing countries. Many politicians in such countries are not knowledgeable (especially how to improve the country's economy) but influential through other means. Many of them do not really care about the country's development; rather just want to stay in power and make money. They are usually good speakers to convince people to get votes or just come to power by force. By providing / acquiring proper information and knowledge, many of such leaders can learn that they can possibly make more money and stay in power longer by changing their policy, attitude and by trying to do some real developments in the country. It is true that most of them do not like to learn on their own; they usually learn through others (e.g. advisors) or when they face some real situation (e.g. recent change in the political system in Egypt which was mainly contributed by social networking). It is believed that with the information access and observing how the world is changing through contributions from the Internet, they will learn it soon and will become instrumental in doing some real development in their countries.

Other developments

There are various other developments possible when a huge resource is created from the base of the pyramid people. These include Health

System, Judicial System, Communication System, Housing and Urban Development.

Increased World Peace

As discussed, internet can stimulate key informal education to the base of the pyramid population group—people can naturally talk, listen and learn. People will be busy in learning as it will help them in various ways, most importantly improving their economic condition.

Once they learn, become knowledgeable and get jobs, they will be more busy with their jobs and possibly with more continued learning. And hence they will be less interested in doing terrorist activities.

Besides, there are various other key added benefits—once base of the pyramid people get out of the poverty (and some become rich as well), all poverty related issues will be minimized or eliminated totally. Key poverty related issues are terrorism, spreading diseases, committing various social crimes, refugees from the developing world, disruption of law & order, not advancing education, healthcare, social depression and the like. Thus, by letting base of the Pyramid people get out of poverty and help drive global economy will in turn greatly help achieve **global peace**.

Chapter 10

What can happen after
the World Economy is Reshaped?
—The Dream, Challenge and Reality

"We know what we are, but we know not what we may become"
—*William Shakespeare*

It is always good to have some good dreams. As we know imagination drives many good things. But to make dreams realistic, we would need to have dreams that are not just very high level imaginations but something that are achievable. Thus, by making the dreams achievable we should be able to make them predictable to a good extent.

Although realistic & achievable dreams are arguably easier to predict, prediction in general is a very difficult problem in nature. It is even more difficult to predict something that would be completely new. So, the predictions made in this chapter may not be correct—but predictions are predictions and we just need to make them using the best possible available knowledge and analysis. Good predictions can help many people to see the future in a different way and may help them come up with new ideas, innovation and entrepreneurship which in return will further help economic, social, cultural, political and other developments with increased world peace as highly emphasized in this book. By the way, this is true even if some predictions will be proved wrong. This is because, wrong predictions will enable some people to make the right predictions and make things better in the long run!

But before making some predictions, let me quickly summarize what is said so far.

In this world of over 6.5 billion people, more than 4 billion people are poor—40% live in poverty, and 16% live in extreme poverty. Many efforts have been going on to alleviate the poverty and minimize the rich-poor gap. One such notable effort is taken by the United Nations. This is called the Millennium Development Goals (MDG). Many people are working together to achieve this worthwhile global dream by 2015.

The poverty is related to various types of gaps including gap in natural resources, gap in ethnicity, gap in male-female capabilities, gap due to the computer revolution (the so called Digital Divide), gap due to disabilities and so on. Broadly speaking, the inequality is inherent in mother-nature. The world natural resources were not uniformly distributed when the world was created, different races were born in different parts of the world inheriting different resources and opportunities, not every human is born with same capabilities, not every human develops same level of intelligence even under "same" environment etc etc. In short, by birth we are all different, the equity is different from the beginning. So, as we grew as a human race more gaps and inequities got developed.

Should we try to reduce all these gaps? Can we really make these gaps go away? If so, how can we do so? These are the few key issues we have addressed. We have discussed that not all gaps can be minimized to the same level but our efforts should be continued to minimize all gaps as much as possible. We then specifically focused on the gap due to the Digital Divide, as it can be reduced to a manageable level that will have a measurable impact on various on-going efforts to reduce the gap between rich and poor.

We have shown that the existing approaches of bridging the Digital Divide are good but not sufficient to truly bridge the Digital Divide. The existing approaches of bridging the Digital Divide can be broadly classified into two groups:

(a) by providing computers or low cost simple computers or computer like devices and Internet connectivity to people who do not have one

(b) by providing personal devices like PDA and cell phone with Internet connectivity

We then provided a practical solution of bridging the Digital Divide by using Voice Internet that uses user's voice and any phone. We have also shown how Voice Internet also bridges the Language Divide and complements existing approaches of bridging the Digital Divide. Voice Internet also removes most of the issues associated with the existing approaches by not requiring to re-write the websites, by providing rendering capability that allows anyone to find short, precise, easily navigable and meaningful desired content in real time while mobile, and by not requiring any need for literacy.

We then have gone beyond just bridging the Digital & Language Divides, and focused on **education, innovation and entrepreneurship** which in turn will create a **huge very useful skilled people (resource)** that can not only help improve their own economy but also help improve the world economy. It will also help social, cultural, political and other developments worldwide in a sustainable way. We have shown that the rich can use newly developed highly skilled brains of the poor to get even richer by investing in this vast human resource. They (have-nots) may be poor from financial standpoint but not from intelligence standpoint. Their brains are as good as many good brains on the "have" side. Bridging the Digital Divide will provide these people more freedom, better economy and social status. More freedom will in turn make them more innovative.

We have also shown that existing free market economy is great but it will continue increasing the gap between the rich and poor as it has been doing for a long time. Something else needs to be done to really minimize the rich-poor gap. We have proposed that our model of creating a huge resource from the bottom of the pyramid people with focus on education, innovation and entrepreneurship would ensure substantial amount of money flow from the rich to the poor in a natural way, and thus can help minimize the rich-poor gap and help achieve MDGs sooner.

Of course we would need to set our expectations right. Many new comers will take some time to come up to speed. Besides, the already rich (both financially and intelligence-wise) people will keep on inventing new things and get richer and so it might be difficult for the new comers to catch or overcome the rich from many aspects. **Even if they catch up or even surpass, there would be no real issue as there is no limit to innovation—rich will come up with various new innovations. So, in turn, all will be benefited driving a new world of prosperity with much lower gap between the rich and poor, and with significantly increased global peace.**

Why increased global peace? Well, once base of the pyramid people get out of the poverty (and some become rich as well), all poverty related issues will be minimized or eliminated totally. Key poverty related issues are terrorism, spreading diseases, committing various social crimes, refugees from the developing world, disruption of law & order, not advancing education, healthcare, social depression and the like. Thus, by enabling base of the Pyramid people to get out of poverty and help drive global economy will in turn greatly help achieve **global peace**.

Now that I have provided a summary of what is described in this book, let me make some predictions (as related to the topics covered in this book):

1. *Through Internet access and informal education, many Base (bottom) of the pyramid people (BOP) will come out of poverty via entrepreneurship and innovation by solving some of their exiting problems.*
2. *Major improvements will be in agriculture and agriculture related products and services.*
3. *Next key improvement will be in e-Learning, mostly informal education.*
4. *Next key improvement will be in e-Commerce.*
5. *Outsourcing will increase rapidly to the base of the pyramid people.*
6. *BOP will start developing new products & services in 2-5 years after Digital & Language Divides are bridged.*
7. *BOP will play a key part in global economy but global economy will still be controlled by the rich. In other words, Base of the*

> *Pyramid people will only be able to truly control world economy when they become rich.*

8. *There will be more rich people at the Base of the Pyramid.*
9. *BOP will develop products for the global market.*
10. *BOP will solve some of their key problems—alternate energy, water, food production.*
11. *BOP will significantly contribute in innovation, especially for problems related to them.*
12. *Through automated Language Translation, BOP people around the world will talk to each other. This will also be true for any people.*
13. *Rich-poor gap will be minimized significantly to a level than what current efforts would be able to do, but rich-poor gap will never go away as it is part of the process of stability.*
14. *In addition to the Economic development, there will be other developments including Social, Cultural and Political.*
15. *There will be significantly increased world peace because of all the above mentioned developments.*

Challenges, Opportunities and Realities:

The approaches and solutions proposed in this book will undoubtedly help the Base of the Pyramid people to help improve their economic, social, cultural, political and other developments. By doing so, they will become active players in the global economy. Money will flow in a major way from rich to the Base of the Pyramid people. As mentioned above, they will do many outsourcing, develop new products and services, some of which will be sold to the global markets.

However, we need to also recognize that the top of the pyramid rich people will still be in the driver seat as they still will remain the major investors, they will be the one who will outsource to the Base of the Pyramid people, they are the one who will also buy from the Base of the Pyramid people. The rich people (including corporations) will still be inventing many new products and services and will remain ahead. **But this is not bad—in fact this is a good win-win situation.** We cannot just expect that poor people will suddenly become rich and control world economy. But they will be much richer than before and some of them will become rich by doing some great innovations so that they can sell it to the global market efficiently. Thus, to really control the world, poor would need to become really rich and innovative. This is something we need to realize.

Now, the situation can be even better. According to many futurists, Economic Growth is Exponential and Accelerating as shown in Fig. 10.1 [LinkTheFuturist].

Fig. 10.1 shows exponential progress in the economy starting at 100 years from year 2000. Today, the US economy grows at a median rate of 3.5% per year, and the world economy at around 4.5% per year. This is a growth rate is expected to continue the same way.
But such annual growth rates were unheard of in the 19th century, or the 18th century (when the world economy grew less than 1% per year). Things changed very little over the span of 1000 or 200 years as show in the graph. People expected their children to have the same living standards, and be surrounded by the same technology, as they were.

Historical World Per Capita GGP

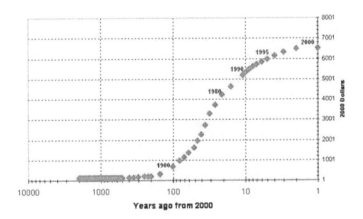

Fig. 10.1 Accelerating Rate of Economic Growth. Courtesy—The Futurists

As indicated in Fig. 10.1, thousands of years of human civilization before the 20th century produced modest wealth compared to what was produced in the much shorter interval of the 20th century. Even with the 20th century, growth was more in the latter half than in the first 50 years.

Now, in 2006, 4% a year is assumed, and taken for granted. In fact, 3 billion people in the world are living in economies growing at greater than 6% a year (China, India, Russia, Vietnam, Pakistan, Thailand, Malaysia, and others).

This would have been considered amazing, at any other time in history. The natural question is, "is this just an aberration, or has the trendline itself shifted, and can we expect this to continue, or even accelerate, in the future?"

In fact, The Futurists [LinkTheFuturist] mentions that this growth is not just exponential, but exponential even in the second derivative i.e. the rate of increase also increases at ever-faster rates . . . .

Of course, it would be great if this prediction becomes true. Question is *"can this be materialized realistically?"*

CAUTION:

I believe such growth cannot continue forever. Why? Because as a human being, our desire are controlled by our biological design. There is a limit on how many new technologies or devices/gadgets we can take every year, how much we can eat everyday, how much medicine we can take everyday, how much salary can increase per year and so on. So, if companies keep on developing new products at an accelerated rate, the consumption will be slowed down eventually and so will be the economic growth.

Also, there are quite a few systems in this world that are difficult to model and hence difficult to predict. Economics is one such area. Existing models and algorithms are based on most off the shelf algorithms and mathematical models. These are great algorithms and models as they have been successfully used solving many real world problems. However, we got to keep in mind that most of today's modeling algorithms are based mainly on physical world problems, especially, focusing on Physics and Chemistry. Although at the *molecular/atomic level quantum mechanics plays important role, rich quantum mechanics have been developed and there are many similarities with Physics and Biology at the molecular/atomic level, **biological cells, systems and humans are still far different from non-biological physical systems, as these have life and life processing elements.** Thus, we would need **a new paradigm to more effectively** model biological cells and systems. Since humans are biological systems and economic behavior is strongly related to human behavior, in addition to existing mathematical equations and models, we **would need good reasoning and possibly new mathematics inspired by observing and understanding biological systems to make better economic predictions.** Moreover, the new understanding that may come from the experiments at Hadron collider research would be useful.*

With such accelerated growth, the Base of the Pyramid people will have a key advantage as they will be able to produce at a lower cost as validated by impressive economic growth by China, India, Malaysia and Thailand.

Another key advantage that Base of the Pyramid people will have is their scalable innovation and entrepreneurial capabilities. Since their number is very large and they will learn the key formula to succeed, they should be able to grow much faster, especially, in developing innovative new products and services that can be sold globally. It is important to note that just by doing outsourcing NO nation can reach to the top as such a nation will depend on someone else who will outsource. To be on the top, a nation would need to develop some creative new things (technologies, products and services) that it can sell very successfully in the global market. So, there is more opportunities and hope for the Base of the Pyramid people!

References

[Bornstein 2005] Bornstein, David, "How to Change the World: Social Entrepreneur and the Power of New Ideas", Oxford University Press and Penguin Books, India, 2004, 2005.

[Bracey2005] B. Bracey et al, "Harnessing the Potential of ICT for Education", UN ICT Task Force Series 9, ISBN 92-1-104548-7.

[Fortune2008] Fortune Magazine, April 4, 2008 Issue, "Muhammad Yunus on tech, profit and the poor", http://money.cnn.com/2008/04/01/technology/muhammed_yunas.fortune/index.htm?source=yahoo_quote

[G@idICT2007] A Publication from UN Global Alliance for ICT Development, New York.

[Hawkins2004] Hawkins, Jeff, "On Intelligence", Times Books, 2004.

[Jurafsky2010] D. Jurafsky et al, "Speech and Language Processing", Prentice Hall, 2010.

[Khan2011] Khan E, "Natural Language Understanding Using Brain-Like Approach: Word Objects and Word Semantics Based Approaches help Sentence Level Understanding", Patent Application, March 2011.

[Khan2010] Khan, E, "Effective Citizen Engagement For Economic & Social Development Using Voice Internet: *Fastest & Practical Way to Bridge Digital & Language Divides*", WSIS Forum, Geneva, May 2010.

[Khan2004] E. Khan, "Outsourcing to Bangladesh: making it a reality", AABEA 2004 Convention, Nov 2004, Silicon Valley, CA, USA.

[Khan2008] E. Khan, "Let Base of the Pyramid People Drive Development through Education, Innovation and Entrepreneurship", Bangladesh Development Initiative, **Democracy and Development in Bangladesh Forum** and The Ash Institute for Democratic Governance & Innovation, JFK School of Government at Harvard University, July 13-14, 2008.

Khan2009ITU] E. Khan, "Very Affordable and Easy to Use Internet for Everyone using any Phone: Ensuring Social Inclusion for People with Disabilities", ITU Asia-Pacific Forum, Aug 25-27, 2009, Bangkok, Thailand.

[Khan2009InfoPoverty] E. Khan, "Internet For Developing World: Fighting Poverty and Enabling Development using Voice Internet", InfoPoverty Conference by OCCAM (a United Nation's affiliated Agency), New York, USA, March 19, 2009.

[Khan2003] E. Khan, "System and Method for Audio-Only Internet Browsing using a Standard Telephone", U.S. Patent Number 6,606,611, Aug 12, 2003.

[Khan2003] E. Khan, "Internet Access to Anyone Anytime Anywhere using natural Voice Over Any Phone", Proceeding of AVIOS, May 2000.

[Khan2007] E. Khan, "How Users are Talking & Listening to the Internet Using Any Phone", Proceeding, CSUN 2007, March, 2007.

[Khan2005] E. Khan, "Internet For Everyone Using Any phone, Without a Computer", Proceeding, CSUN 2005, March, 2005.

[Lewis2007] H. Lewis, "Are Rich Necessary", Axios Press, 2007.

[Polak2008] Polak, Paul, "Out of Poverty", Berret-Koehler Publishers, Inc., 2008.

[Prahlad2004] Prahlad, C.K., "The Fortune at the Bottom of the Pyramid: Eradicating Poverty through Profits", Wharton School Publishing, 2004.

[Sciadas2002] George Sciadas, "Monitoring the Digital Divide", Orbicom 2002: ISBN: 2-922651-01-0, http://www.orbicom.ca/projects/ddi2002/ddi2002.pdf

[Santoyo2003] Santoyo, A, "Estimation and Characterization of the Digital Divide", Round Table on Developing Countries to Scientific

[Skousen1991] Skousen, M, "Economics on Trial: Lies, Myths, and Realities", McGraw Hill, 1991.

[Sen1999] Sen, Amartya, "Development as Freedom", Oxford University Press, 1999.

[Slocum 1985] Slocum, Jonathan, "A survey of Machine Tranlsation: its History, Current Status, and Future Prospects", Computational Lingustics, Volume 11, Number 1, January-March, 1985.

[Stiglitz2006] Stiglitz, J., "Making Globalization Work", W.W. Norton & Company, 2006.

[Yunus2007] Yunus, Muhammad et al, "Creating a World Without Poverty", PublicAffairs, 2007.

Key Links

[LinkMDG] Millennium Development Goals (MDG), http://www.un.org/millenniumgoals/statements.shtml

[LinkIDE] IDE (International Development Enterprise)—www.ide-international.rg

[LinkSTAT]http://www.statcan.gc.ca/pub/56f0004m/56f0004m2002007-eng.pdf
ISBN: 0-662-32226-6

[LinkORBICOM] "From Digital Divide to Digital Opportunities", Claude Yves Charron, Orbicom, 2005—http://www.itu.int/ITU-D/ict/publications/dd/material/index_ict_opp.pdf

[LinkMDD] "Monitoring the Digital Divide", Presentation at ITU-Kado Digtal Bridges Symposium, Busan, Korea, Sept 2004.

[LinkSCALING]http://www.hks.harvard.edu/pepg/PDF/events/colloquia/Vigdor_ScalingtheDigitalDivide.pdf

[LinkWAVE]http://doc.openfing.org/FING/LAFING/PUBLICATIONS/Serrano.pdf—1st wave to 4th wave as a reference

[LinkUNCTAD]http://www.unctad.org/Templates/Webflyer.asp?docID=6531&intItemID=3369&lang=1&print=1—UNCTAD & ITU to measure the magnitude of the Divide, as a reference (took initiative in Nov 2005)

[LinkNGRAM] n-gram trillion dataset http://googleresearch.blogspot.com/2006/08/all-our-n-gram-are-belong-to-you.html

[LinkOCCAM] www.occam.org

[LinkInfoPoverty] www.infopoverty.net

[LinkInfoPovertyFoundation] www.InfoPovertyFoundation.com

[LinkWSISKhan2010]http://www.itu.int/wsis/implementation/2010/forum/geneva/tw/tw_12.html

[LinkWSIS] http://www.itu.int/wsis/index.html

[LinkITU] http://www.itu.int/en/pages/default.aspx

[LinkITUKhan2009] http://www.itu.int/ITU-D/asp/CMS/Events/2009/PwDs/programme.asp

[LinkG3ICT] http://www.g3ict.org/

[LinkTRANSLATION]http://en.wikipedia.org/wiki/
Wikipedia:Translation

[LinkALLDIVIDES]http://t06.cgpublisher.com/proposals/161/index
html—combines all the Divides (Digital, Rich/poor etc and makes it
complicated)

[LinkJOBS]http://www.fastcompany.com/magazine/118/
unplanned-obsolescence.html
"Innovation distinguishes a leader from a follower"—Steve Jobs

[LinkMangoPreserve1]http://in.answers.yahoo.com/question/
index?qid=20070606073623AAuiNPV

[LinkMangoPreserve2]http://www.ehow.com/how_2290050_
make-mango-preserve.html

[LinkMagoPreserve3] http://www.indianexpress.com/news/honey-the-
new-mantra-for-mango-preservation/433791/

[LinkUnix] http://en.wikipedia.org/wiki/Unix

[LinkTheFuturist] http://www.wfs.org/futurist

[LinkInternetWorldStats] http://www.internetworldstats.com/stats.htm

[LinkCBSNews] http://www.cbsnews.com/stories/2010/02/15/business/
main6209772.shtml

[LinkGlobalIssues]http://www.globalissues.org/article/26/
poverty-facts-and-stats

[LinkExtensionServices_2_Bangladesh] http://www.unnayan.org/
reports/agri/AgricultureExt.pdf

[LinkExtensionService_1_Wiki]http://en.wikipedia.org/wiki/
Cooperative_extension_service

[LinkExtensionService_1_Mozambique]http://jae.oxfordjournals.org/content/early/2011/05/19/jae.ejr015.short?rss=1

[LinkUNICEF_Zambia] http://www.unicef.org/infobycountry/zambia_statistics.html

[LinkEISA_Zambia] http://www.eisa.org.za/WEP/zam1.htm

APPENDIX A

Agricultural Extensions

Since agriculture is one of the key focus areas for bottom of the pyramid people and since we have emphasized on using Voice Internet for Agricultural Extensions strongly, this appendix is added to provide more details on Agricultural Extensions and how Voice Internet can significantly increase its usage and effectiveness. Traditional Extension Services are not available (or available to a limited extent) in many underdeveloped and developing countries. Voice Internet makes such Extension Services available via any phone, thus making such services available to anyone having some access to any phone. The same concept applies for various other e-services including e-Learning, e-Gov, and e-Health.

What is Agricultural Extension Service

Agricultural extension service basically means providing and educating farmers with key information about agriculture through various institutions and organizations. The word "extension" is used as most of the key information and latest findings about agriculture are mainly available at various universities and research institutions; and thus these need to be provided to (i.e. extended to) the farmers and other associated people mainly in rural areas. The following quote from Wikipedia [LinkExtensionService_1_Wiki] explains this further:

"Agricultural extension was once known as the application of scientific research and new knowledge to agricultural practices through farmer education. The field of extension now encompasses a wider range of communication and learning activities organized for rural people by professionals from different disciplines, including agriculture, agricultural marketing, health, and business studies."

Providers and Supporters of Agricultural Extension Services

There are various types of organizations providing extension services. These include NGOs, Governments / Government Agencies (e.g. USAID—United States Agency for International Development), and other organizations e.g. APEN (Australasia-Pacific Extension Network). Most providers are supported by various government agencies.

Besides, there are various associated supporting institutions & networks such as AGREN (The Agricultural Research and Extension Network), and extension journals such as Journal of Extension *(JOE)*.

Agricultural extension agencies in developing countries have received large amounts of support from international development organizations such as the World Bank and the Food and Agriculture Organization (FAO) of the United Nations.

How Communication takes place in an Extension System [LinkExtensionService_1_Wiki]

There are various ways communications takes place—two major widely accepted ones are:

- systems of communication that aim to change the behavior of rural people
- systems of communication that aim to change the knowledge of rural people

There is, of course, a close relationship between knowledge and behavior; changes in the former often lead to a change in the latter.

If government policy-makers, project managers or researchers direct the topics addressed and projects undertaken, then the purpose of extension is to change behavior. If farmers and other rural people direct the extension towards their own needs, then the purpose of extension is changing knowledge. This knowledge helps rural people make their own decisions regarding farming practices. This approach to extension is closely related to *non-formal education* and generating awareness.

Such communications usually focuses on Technology Transfer, Advisory Work, Human Resource Development and facilitation for empowerment.

How Effective are Extension Services [LinkExtensionService_1_ Mozambique], [LinkExtensionServices_2_Bangladesh]

Extension services have been effective in many developed and some developing countries. For many underdeveloped and developing countries, the effectiveness has been significantly limited for various reasons including limited manpower (e.g. limited number of extension officers or even no extension service providing personnel), limited funding, lack of coordination between the government and extension practitioners, lack of cooperation to augment effectiveness, duplication and wastage of scarce resources, farmers bad experience on extension services and hence less motivation and enthusiasm. Besides, in many underdeveloped and developing countries the number of extension service practitioners is very few or no extension services are available at all.

Thus, even though all related parties are very interested and possibly try their best to help various extension service initiatives, the result has been limited and there is room for significant improvement.

How Voice Internet can help Improve Extension Services

As stated, one key reason for limited effectiveness of extension services is cost and associated funding. Another key reason is lack of communication between all related parties including the farmers. By providing Voice Internet based on-line extension services, these key issues can be addressed very effectively. Voice Internet can bring the cost down significantly as farmers will get all key information from some Farming Extension Portals by calling a phone number from any phone, and then learning about key agriculture related topics by just talking and listening. Through interaction using the natural user interface (i.e. talking and listening) from a ubiquitous device (a simple phone), farmers will learn most up to date information fast. They will also be able to easily share (e.g. via email, Social Network websites like Facebook and Twitter) their experience with fellow farmers; thus improve and enhance their understanding about new approaches, technologies very easily. Extension service practitioners and all supporting institutions and organizations can also help significantly in various ways e.g. by designing various Extension Service Portals and putting more appropriate content. The farmers will also be able to learn more by learning how to use general Internet features (like surfing, email, searching and more). This will enable them to increase their production, minimize waste (e.g. by learning how to preserve), and also start selling online to the buyers directly; thus bypassing the middlemen and increasing their ROI (Return on Investment). This will in turn help governments as governments will be able to export more with higher margin, and thus help improving the GDP (Gross Domestic Product). Many farmers will be able to start new farming related businesses. Refer to Chapter 8 and Chapter 9 for some examples.

Because phone service is widely available, Voice Internet based extension services will significantly increase the outreach at a very low cost. As already emphasized by many experts, informal education is very important for farmers. Voice Internet based informal education would be much simpler and effective as it does not require literacy (one just talks and listen), and interactive self-learning is much simpler & easier. Since most of the farmers are illiterate (hence do not know how to read or write), Voice Internet will significantly ease the learning process.

Voice Internet based learning also enables them to move up the food chain and come up with new products and services, and start new businesses. Once they become more efficient and improve their ROI, it will be easier for them to get more funding, especially long term loan (or some grants) so that they can expand their businesses in various ways and employ more people. E.g. some of the farmers would be able to learn enough to provide some key extension services face to face to those who may not be very comfortable to learn via phone (shyness, inertia to not learn anything new etc) or they can start new companies doing low cost Food Preservation and thus minimizing waste (see Chapter 9 for some examples).

Above mentioned approaches with Voice Internet also work well for other applications including training in "village chicken commercial production" methods and use of its manure for bio gas energy production for lighting and cooking.

In summary, Voice Internet based Extension Services

1. Provide basic farming related education to all farmers via any phone and user's voice (see some examples in Chapter 9).
2. Provide many farming applications via on-line using any phone.
3. Help farmers sell more easily via simple selling outlets.
4. Help farmers sell via online shopping portals.
5. Help farmers learn how to minimize waste and preserve their produce by converting them into various processed food products (see Chapter 9 for details).
6. Help get funding through Voice Internet based Microfinance (see Chapter 9 for details).
7. Help them to move up the food chain and come up with new forms of products and services, and start new businesses.

Index

www.ingramcontent.com/pod-product-compliance
Lightning Source LLC
LaVergne TN
LVHW042137040326
832903LV00011B/279/J